The Book of Insults

To my family, without whose solicitous concern and helpful suggestions this book would have been finished in half the time.

The Book of Insults Ancient & Modern

An Amiable History of Insult, Invective,
Imprecation & Incivility (Literary,
Political & Historical) Hurled Through
the Ages & Compiled as a Public Service
by Nancy McPhee

Futura

Futura

First published in Great Britain by Paddington
Press in 1978
First Futura Publications edition 1980
11th printing 1990

ISBN: 0 7088 1907 9

Printed in Great Britain by
Richard Clay Ltd, Bungay, Suffolk

Futura Publications
A division of
Macdonald & Co (Publishers) Ltd
Orbit House, 1 New Fetter Lane, London
EC4A 1AR
A member of Maxwell Macmillan Pergamon Publishing Corporation

Contents

A collector of quotations inevitably has some of the qualities of a parasite, feeding off the labors of others. Many of the verbal tidbits in this book have appeared in a large number of other works, often in frustratingly different variants; although I am no scholar, I have done my best to track down the original wordings and sources. Should any material regrettably have been used without proper permission, amendment will be made in the future editions which popular acclaim will no doubt demand. For the rest, I must be content to tip my hat to my many forerunners, breathe a fervent word of thanks for their work, and fall back on the dictum of Wilson Mizner:

If you steal from one author, it's plagiarism;

if you steal from many, it's research.

N.G.M.

The Author wishes to thank the following for permission to reprint material included in this book: Sir Rupert Hart-Davis for extracts by Max Beerbohm. Harper & Row Publishers Inc. for extracts by Robert Benchley. The Estate of the late E.C. Bentley and A.P. Watt Ltd. for extracts from two poems "Geoffrey Chaucer" and "George the Third" by E.C. Bentley. George Allen & Unwin Ltd. and Barnes & Noble for extracts from *Letters From England* by Karel Capek. William Heinemann Ltd. for extracts from *The Life and Letters of Sir Edmond Gosse* by Evan Charteris. Dodd, Mead & Co. and A.P. Watt Ltd. for two lines of poetry by G.K. Chesterton. John Robert Colombo for extracts from *Colombo's Concise Canadian Quotations*, Edmonton: Hurtig Publishers, 1976, and "Oh Canada" from *The Sad Truths*, Toronto: Peter Martin Associates, 1974. Syndication International Ltd. for extracts from *Boiled Cabbage* by William Connor. PMA Books for extracts from *I Never Say Anything Provocative*, edited by Margaret Wente (1975). Simon & Schuster, a Division of Gulf & Western Corporation, for extracts from *With Malice Toward Some* by Margaret Halsey (Copyright © 1938, 1965 by Margaret Halsey). The Sterling Lord Agency, Inc. for extracts from *The Fine Art of Political Wit* by Leon A. Harris. The Society of Authors as literary representative of the Estate of A.E. Houseman for extracts from A.E. Houseman's work. *The Washington Post* for extracts by Paul Hume. Mrs. Dorinda Maxse for extracts by Henry Arthur Jones. Clarke, Irwin & Company Ltd. for extracts from *The Firebrand* by William Kilbourn. The National Trust and A.P. Watt Ltd. for extracts from two poems by Rudyard Kipling. Doubleday & Company Inc. for extracts from *The Cutting Edge* by Louis Kronenberger (Copyright © 1970 by Louis Kronenberger). Faber & Faber Ltd. for extracts from *The Whitsun Weddings* by Philip Larkin. The Macmillan Company of Canada Ltd. and Houghton Mifflin Company for the poem "William Lyon Mackenzie King" from *Alligator Pie* by Dennis Lee (Copyright © 1974 by Dennis Lee). The Author and the author's agents, Scott Meredith Literary Agency, Inc., 845 Third Avenue, New York, New York 10022 for extracts from *Some Notes on the 1960 Democratic Convention* by Norman Mailer. The John Hopkins University Press for extracts from *H.L. Mencken, A Carnival of Buncombe* by Malcolm Moos. Curtis Brown, Inc. and Little Brown and Co. for the poem "Further Reflections on Parsley" by Ogden Nash (Copyright © 1942, 1959 by Ogden Nash). Herbert V. Prochnow for extracts from *A Treasury of Humorous Quotations* by Herbert V. Prochnow and Herbert V. Prochnow Jr. George Allen & Unwin Ltd. for extracts from *Sceptical Essays* by Bertrand Russell. Frank R. Scott for an extract from *Selected Poems*. The Society of Authors on behalf of the Bernard Shaw Estate for extracts from Bernard Shaw's work. Mrs Iris Wise, Macmillan, London and Basingstoke. The Macmillan Company of Canada Ltd. and Macmillan Publishing Co. Inc., for an excerpt from *Collected Poems of James Stephens*. The Society of Authors as agents for The Strachey Trust for extracts by Lytton Strachey. The New Yorker Magazine, Inc, for a caption by E.B. White to a cartoon by Carl Rose, Copyright © 1928, 1956 by The New Yorker Magazine, Inc.

Foreword

From time immemorial, men have relished the delights of verbal warfare. It is a paradox of our own inarticulate age that this enjoyment of a clever insult has never been higher. Having largely lost our interest in using language with precision and imagination, we hide our real thoughts behind fuzzy words and a mealy mouth — but we secretly admire those who have the courage to say aloud what we ourselves only dare to think!

No doubt there are profound and Freudian reasons for this malicious pleasure; but whatever the explanation, the immense popularity of television and nightclub comedians who specialize in the blunt put-down demonstrates that verbal violence strikes a deep and responsive chord. The sad fact that so many of these performers are graceless and vulgar does not seem to lessen their appeal, although it does highlight a deplorable decline in the art of invective.

For there was a golden age, not so long ago, when insult was indeed an art; when people had strong opinions and were only too ready to voice them. Over the years there have been many who called a spade a spade with imagination, wit and style.

This modest collection of boos and catcalls has tried to bring together some of the best of these. Connoisseurs of the art will recognize many famous broadsides, and note the absence of others. My choices were highly personal and no doubt eccentric. What they have in common is a deft and uninhibited use of language, all too often missing today.

Still, those of us who cherish this black side of literature should not be too pessimistic. There are enough contemporary examples of inventive insult to encourage the hope that the tide may yet be turned. If this collection can both amuse and inspire its readers to a more creative use of invective, it will have served its purpose.

N.G.M.
1978

HIS MIND WAS LIKE
A SOUP DISH—
WIDE AND SHALLOW...
IRVING STONE ON
WM. JENNINGS BRYAN

I'LL TICKLE YOUR CATASTROPHE

*A*way, you scullion! you rampallion!
you fustilarian! I'll tickle your catastrophe.

William Shakespeare (1564-1616)
King Henry IV, Second Part

Throughout the centuries, human beings have exercized their highest powers of invention and wit in speaking ill of one another. That leaven of malice which exists in all of us has been exalted in some people almost to the point of genius; and thousands of otherwise amiable souls have risen to the occasional pointed put-down or audacious phrase which the world has relished enough to note and long remember.

One can turn to the Bible for inspiration in many things — among them, the use of a rather mild form of invective:

> *O generation of vipers, who hath warned you to flee from the wrath to come?*
>
> Matthew 3:7

> *Ye blind guides, which strain at a gnat, and swallow a camel.*
>
> Matthew 23:24

> *Because thou art lukewarm and neither cold nor hot, I will spue thee out of my mouth.*
>
> Revelations 3:16

> *A whip for the horse, a bridle for the ass, and a rod for the fool's back.*
>
> Proverbs 26:3

The ancient Romans were never afraid to be uncomplimentary; the poet Martial made a career of it:

> *I could do without your face, Chloë, and without your neck, and your hands, and your limbs, and, to*

*save myself the trouble of mentioning the points in
detail, I could do without you altogether.*
Marcus Valerius Martial (c.40-104 AD)

*Nycilla dyes her locks, 'tis said,
But 'tis a foul aspersion;
She buys them black; they therefore need
No subsequent immersion.*
Marcus Valerius Martial (c.40-104 AD)

Strong language has always sat well in the mouths of
strong and powerful men. One such person with firm
opinions and a caustic tongue was King James I of
England. James, who considered himself an expert in a
variety of fields, earnestly attempted to suppress a habit
which has yet to be wiped out by a succession of similar
exhortations:

> *... And for the vanities committed in this filthie
> custome, is it not both great vanitie and unclean-
> nesse, that at the table, a place of respect, of
> cleanlinesse, of modestie, men should not be
> ashamed, to sit tossing of Tobacco pipes, and
> puffing of the smoke of Tobacco one to another,
> making the filthy smoke and stinke thereof, to
> exhale athwart the dishes, and infect the aire, when
> very often men that abhorre it are at their repast?
> ... it makes a kitchin also often-times in the inward
> parts of men, soiling and infecting them, with an
> unctuous and oily kinde of Soote, as hath bene
> found in some great Tobacco takers, that after their
> death were opened.*

> *... Have you not reason then to bee ashamed, and
> to forbeare this filthie noveltie ... a custome
> loathsome to the eye, hatefull to the nose, harmefull
> to the braine, dangerous to the Lungs, and in the
> blacke stinking fume thereof, neerest resembling
> the horrible Stigian smoke of the pit that is
> bottomlesse.*
King James I of England (1566-1625)
A Counterblaste to Tobacco

Invective and abuse turns up in even less likely places than the essays of a scholar-king. The man who imported tobacco into Europe, Sir Walter Raleigh, met a sticky end: for this and other sins he was hanged, drawn and quartered. Such harsh punishment may have come almost as a relief after his subjection, during his trial, to this incredible tirade:

> *I will prove you the notoriousest traitor that ever came to the bar. ... thou art a monster; thou hast an English face, but a Spanish heart. ... Thou art the most vile and execrable Traitor that ever lived. ... I want words sufficient to express thy viperous Treasons.... Thou art an odious fellow, thy name is hateful to all the realm of England. ... There never lived a viler viper upon the face of the earth than thou.*

Sir Edward Coke (1552-1634)
To Sir Walter Raleigh

Such verbal pyrotechnics were by no means rare. One of the joys of true invective, for both practitioner and audience, is the opportunity for the imagination to soar in flights of bombast. Some creative critics have been punch-drunk with words:

> *Cut-purses, miles of cheats, enterprises of scoundrels, delicious disgusts, foolish decisions, crippled hopes, virile women, effeminate men, and everywhere the love of gold.*

Giordano Bruno (c.1548-1600)
On his life and times

> *You common cry of curs! whose breath I hate*
> *As reek o' the rotten fens, whose loves I prize*
> *As the dead carcases of unburied men*
> *That do corrupt the air.*

William Shakespeare (1564-1616)
Coriolanus

> *Vain Nashe, railing Nashe, cracking Nashe, bibbing Nashe, baggage Nashe, swaddish Nashe, roguish Nashe ... the swish-swash of the press, the bum of impudency, the shambles of beastliness*

... the toadstool of the realm. ...
Gabriel Harvey (1545-1630)
On Thomas Nashe

The gentle Charles Lamb suffered the sad fate of many a playwright when his new play was hissed on its first night. So violent was the audience's reaction that Lamb joined in the hissing himself, lest he be mistaken for the author! Describing the scene to a friend, Lamb later unleashed an uncharacteristic torrent of venom:

> *Mercy on us, that God should give his favourite children, men, mouths to speak with, discourse rationally, to promise smoothly, to flatter agreeably, to encourage warmly, to counsel wisely: to sing with, to drink with, and to kiss with: and that they should turn them into mouths of adders, bears, wolves, hyenas, and whistle like tempests, and emit breath through them like distillations of aspic poison, to asperse and vilify the innocent labour of their fellow creatures who are desirous to please them. God be pleased to make the breath stink and the teeth rot out of them all therefore!*

Charles Lamb (1775-1834)

One of the greatest comic characters in all literature, Sir John Falstaff, had his many deficiencies catalogued by his creator:

> *Why dost thou converse with that trunk of humours, that bolting-hutch of beastliness, that swoln parcel of dropsies, that huge bombard of sack, that stuffed cloakbag of guts, that roasted Manningtree ox with the pudding in his belly, that reverend vice, that grey iniquity, that father ruffian, that vanity in years?*

William Shakespeare (1564-1616)
King Henry IV, Second Part

Some fastidious cursers discover that words in common use cannot express their incoherent anger—they take refuge in the obscure, or even make up their own!

A blatant Bassarid of Boston, a rampant Maenad of Massachusetts.

Algernon Swinburne (1837-1909)
On Harriet Beecher Stowe

This dodipoule, this didopper... Why, thou arrant butter whore, thou cotqueane & scrattop of scoldes, wilt thou never leave afflicting a dead Carcasse... a wispe, a wispe, rippe, rippe, you kitchin-stuff wrangler!

Thomas Nashe (1567-1601)
On Gabriel Harvey

A gap-toothed and hoary-headed ape ... who now in his dotage spits and chatters from a dirtier perch of his own finding and fouling: coryphaeus or choragus of his Bulgarian tribe of autocoprophagous baboons ...

Algernon Swinburne (1837-1909)
On Ralph Waldo Emerson

A freakish homunculus germinated outside lawful procreation.

Henry Arthur Jones (1851-1929)
On Bernard Shaw

A Byzantine logothete.

Theodore Roosevelt (1858-1919)
On Woodrow Wilson

Calling them slubberdegullion druggles ... ninny lobcocks, scurvy sneaksbies ... noddy meacocks, blockish grutnols, doddi-pol jolt-heads, jobbernol goosecaps ... flutch calf-lollies, grouthead gnatsnappers, lob-dotterels... codshead loobies, ninnie-hammer fly-catchers ... and other such like defamatory epithets.

François Rabelais (c. 1490-1553)

A warts-and-all description of a person's physical characteristics has always been an effective way of being unpleasant:

With leering Looks, Bull-fac'd, and freckl'd fair,
With two left legs, and Judas-color'd Hair,

And frowzy Pores that taint the ambient Air.

John Dryden (1631-1700)
On Jacob Tonson, a publisher

They brought one Pinch, a hungry lean-fac'd
*   villain,*
A mere anatomy, a mountebank,
A threadbare juggler, and a fortune-teller,
A needy, hollow-ey'd, sharp-looking wretch,
A living dead man.

William Shakespeare (1564-1616)
The Comedy of Errors

Why don't you get a haircut? You look like a
chrysanthemum.

P.G. Wodehouse (1881-1975)

He's a little man, that's his trouble. Never trust
a man with short legs—brains too near their
bottoms.

Noel Coward (1899-1973)

Other naysayers can describe their victims almost tangibly with the word-pictures they draw:

The English country-gentleman galloping after
a fox—the unspeakable in full pursuit of the
uneatable.

Oscar Wilde (1854-1900)

His mind is a muskeg of mediocrity.

John Macnaughton (1858-1943)
On an anonymous Canadian professor

A louse in the locks of literature.

Alfred, Lord Tennyson (1809-1894)
On critic Churton Collins

His mind was like a soup dish, wide and shallow;
it could hold a small amount of nearly anything,
but the slightest jarring spilled the soup into
somebody's lap.

Irving Stone (b. 1903)
On William Jennings Bryan

O hideous little bat, the size of snot.

> Karl Shapiro (b. 1913)
> *The Fly*

His mind was a kind of extinct sulphur-pit.

> Thomas Carlyle (1795-1881)
> On Napoleon III

He was the mildest manner'd man
That ever scuttled ship or cut a throat.

> Lord Byron (1788-1824)

He is like trying to pick up mercury with a fork.

> Lloyd George (1863-1945)
> On Eamon de Valera

My handwriting looks as if a swarm of ants, escaping from an ink bottle, had walked over a sheet of paper without wiping their legs.

> Sydney Smith (1771-1845)

Subtler souls find the gentle touch effective:

Why do you sit there looking like an envelope without any address on it?

> Mark Twain (1835-1910)

I like him and his wife. He is so ladylike, and she is such a perfect gentleman.

> Sydney Smith (1771-1845)

To mankind in general, Macbeth and Lady Macbeth stand out as the supreme type of all that a host and hostess should not be.

> Max Beerbohm (1872-1956)

Funny without being vulgar.

> Sir Herbert Beerbohm
> Tree (1853-1917)
> On his own performance as Hamlet

You and I were long friends; you are now my enemy, and I am

> *Yours,*
> *B. Franklin*

> Benjamin Franklin (1706-1790)
> Letter to William Strahan

Still others enjoy a play on words:

He has impeccable bad taste.

Otis Ferguson

Very nice, though there are dull stretches.

Antoine de Rivarol (1753-1801)
On a two-line poem

If only he'd wash his neck, I'd wring it.

John Sparrow

The man who could call a spade a spade should be compelled to use one. It is the only thing he is fit for.

Oscar Wilde (1854-1900)

The tightly-knit literary and artistic communities of the past often led to strong personal animosities and yielded a rich vein of personal abuse:

Of course we all know that Morris was a wonderful all-round man, but the act of walking round him has always tired me.

Max Beerbohm (1872-1956)
On William Morris

Rossini would have been a great composer if his teacher had spanked him enough on his backside.

Ludwig van Beethoven (1770-1827)

Poor Matt. He's gone to heaven, no doubt—but he won't like God.

Robert Louis Stevenson (1850-1894)
On Matthew Arnold

Henry James was one of the nicest old ladies I ever met.

William Faulkner (1897-1962)

Thackeray settled like a meat-fly on whatever one had got for dinner, and made one sick of it.

John Ruskin (1819-1900)

Every once in a while someone achieved the perfect squelch:

Your manuscript is both good and original; but the

part that is good is not original, and the part that is original is not good.

Samuel Johnson (1709-1784)

You may have genius. The contrary is, of course, probable.

Oliver Wendell Holmes (1841-1935)

From the moment I picked your book up until I laid it down I was convulsed with laughter. Some day I intend reading it.

Groucho Marx (b. 1895)

Periodically, a new art form is invented and turned to unkind uses. E.C. Bentley, the detective-story writer, devised the clerihew:

Geoffrey Chaucer
Took a bath (in a saucer)
In consequence of certain hints
Dropped by the Black Prince.

E. Clerihew Bentley (1875-1956)

The use of the formal curse reaches back into unrecorded history, and is still in vogue in parts of the world today. The mediaeval church laid this heavy imprecation on the heads of its excommunicated sinners:

Let him be damned in his going out and coming in. The Lord strike him with madness and blindness. May the heavens empty upon him thunderbolts and the wrath of the Omnipotent burn itself unto him in the present and future world. May the Universe light against him and the earth open to swallow him up.

Pope Clement VI (1478-1534)

The traditional Gypsy curse chilled Europeans for years:

May you wander over the face of the earth forever, never sleep twice in the same bed, never drink water twice from the same well, and never cross the same river twice in a year.

while curses from esoteric corners of the earth could be bloodcurdling:

> *Die, may he: Tiger, catch him; Snake, bite him;*
> *Steep hill, fall down on him; River, flow over him;*
> *Wild boar, bite him.*
>
> Ceremonial curse of the Todas of India

> *May you dig up your father by moonlight and make*
> *soup of his bones.*
>
> Fiji Islands

or merely uncomfortable:

> *May the fleas of a thousand camels infest your*
> *armpits.*
>
> Arab curse

> *May your left ear wither and fall into your right*
> *pocket.*
>
> Arab curse

> *May you melt off the earth like snow off the ditch.*
>
> Irish curse

> *May the curse of Mary Malone and her nine blind*
> *illegitimate children chase you so far over the hills*
> *of Damnation that the Lord himself can't find you*
> *with a telescope.*
>
> Irish curse

The Chinese and the Scots were struck with the same philosophical thought:

> *May you be born in an important time.*
>
> Confucius (c.551-478 BC)

> *May you live in interesting times.*
>
> Old Scottish curse

and a host of more recent imitators have shown more or less ingenuity:

> *May she marry a ghost, and bear him a kitten, and*
> *may the High King of Glory permit it to get the*
> *mange.*
>
> James Stephens (1882-1950)

*I would thou didst itch from head to foot and I had
the scratching of thee.*

William Shakespeare (1564-1616)
Troilus and Cressida

*May you be cursed with a chronic anxiety about the
weather.*

John Burroughs (1837-1921)

The real test of the creative insult is its use in conversation. Which of us has not thought of the perfect response
— twenty-four hours too late? The witty retort has always
been enjoyed and frequently recorded:

> THE EARL OF SANDWICH: *Egad, sir, I do not know
> whether you will die on the gallows or of the pox.*
> JOHN WILKES: *That will depend, my Lord, on whether
> I embrace your principles or your mistress.*

John Wilkes (1727-1797)

> *
> CLERGYMAN: *How did you like my sermon, Mr.
> Canning?*
> CANNING: *You were brief.*
> CLERGYMAN: *Yes, you know I avoid being tedious.*
> CANNING: *But you* were *tedious.*

George Canning (1770-1827)

The quick-witted responses of Winston Churchill have
become legendary:

> LADY ASTOR: *Winston, if you were my husband, I
> should flavour your coffee with poison.*
> CHURCHILL: *Madam, if I were your husband, I should
> drink it.*
> *
> BESSIE BRADDOCK, M.P.: *Winston, you're drunk!*
> CHURCHILL: *Bessie, you're ugly. And tomorrow
> morning I shall be sober.*

Bernard Shaw once sent Churchill two tickets for the
opening of his new play, with the invitation:

> *Bring a friend — if you have one.*

Churchill regretted that he was engaged, and asked for
tickets for the second performance:

If there is one.

Winston Churchill (1874-1965)

Dorothy Parker was seldom caught with her wits down:

> CLARE BOOTHE LUCE (*meeting Parker in a doorway*):
> *Age before beauty!*
> DOROTHY PARKER (*gliding through the door*): *Pearls
> before swine!*

Dorothy Parker (1893-1967)

To speak ill of the dead is, of course, the ultimate form of insult; and no doubt this is one reason for the popularity of the epitaph. One such relic from mediaeval Italy celebrates a man who was a notorious and vicious gossip:

> *Here lies Aretino, Tuscan poet*
> *Who spoke evil of everyone but God,*
> *Giving the excuse, "I never knew Him."*

Anonymous

Some writers of epitaphs are cutting and cruel; here is Lord Byron on a contemporary politician:

With death doomed to grapple
Beneath this cold slab, he
Who lied in the Chapel
Now lies in the Abbey.

Lord Byron (1788-1824)
On William Pitt

Some are sarcastic, as in this epitaph on an inattentive waiter:

By and by
God caught his eye.

David McCord (b. 1897)

and some are frivolous:

Excuse my dust.

This one's on me.

Dorothy Parker (1893-1967)
Suggested epitaphs

But none of these is as heartfelt as the genuine epitaph on a tombstone in the churchyard at Horsley-Down, Cumberland, erected in less than loving memory to "Mary, wife of Thomas Bond" by her brother-in-law:

She was proud, peevish and passionate ...
Her behaviour was discreet toward strangers
      But
    Independent in her family ...
She was a professed enemy to flattery,
and was seldom known to praise or commend ...
The talents in which she principally excelled
Were difference of opinion, and discovering
    flaws and imperfections ...
She sometimes made her husband happy ...
      But
Much more frequently miserable ...
Insomuch that in 30 years cohabitation he ...
    had not in the whole, enjoyed two years
      of matrimonial comfort.
        At length

> Finding that she had lost the affections of her
>   husband,
>   As well as the regard of her neighbours,
> Family disputes having been divulged by servants,
>   She died of vexation, July 20, 1768
>   Aged 48 years.

The late Mistress Bond was only one of many women who
have been maligned through the ages:

> *She never was really charming till she died.*
>
> Terence (c.185-159 BC)

> *God created Adam lord of all living creatures, but
> Eve spoiled it all.*
>
> Martin Luther (1483-1546)

Many men have shared Luther's opinion about women:

> *Nature intended women to be our slaves. ... they
> are our property; we are not theirs. They belong to
> us, just as a tree that bears fruit belongs to a
> gardener. What a mad idea to demand equality for
> women ! ... Women are nothing but machines for
> producing children.*
>
> Napoleon Bonaparte (1769-1821)

> *A woman is only a woman,*
> *But a good cigar is a smoke.*
>
> Rudyard Kipling (1865-1936)

and have expended a good deal of energy in detailing
their deficiencies:

> *Nature, I say, doth paynt them further to be weak,
> fraile, impacient, feble, and foolishe; and experience
> hath declared them to be unconstant, variable,
> cruell, and lacking the spirit of counsel and regi-
> ment.*
>
> John Knox (1505-1575)
> *The First Blast of the Trumpet Against*
> *the Monstrous Regiment of Women*

> *The five worst infirmities that afflict the female are*

indocility, discontent, slander, jealousy and silliness.

Confucian Marriage Manual

The English Puritans considered their young women to be gad-abouts:

> *The dissolutenesse of our lascivious, impudent, rattle-pated gadding females now is such ... they are lowde and stubborne; their feet abide not in their houses; now they are without, now in the streets, and lie in wait at every corner; being never well pleased nor contented, but when they are wandering abroad to Playes, to Playhouses, Dancing-Matches, Masques, and publicke Shewes.*

William Prynne (1600-1669)

The straight-laced Mr. Prynne was horrified at the modern fashion of shingling women's hair:

> *Even nature herselfe abhors to see a woman shorne or polled; a woman with cut hair is a filthy spectacle, and much like a monster; and all repute it a very great absurdity for a woman to walke abrode with shorne hair; for this is all one as if she should take upon her the forme or person of a man, to whom short cut haire is proper, it being naturall and comly to women to nourish their haire, which even God and nature have given them for a covering, a token of their subjection, and a natural badge to distinguish them from men.*

William Prynne (1600-1669)

And although most men have agreed that marriage is women's proper role in life, they have seldom had a good word to say for it:

> *I have always thought that every woman should marry, and no man.*

Benjamin Disraeli (1804-1881)

> *Strange to say what delight we married people have to see these poor fools decoyed into our condition.*

Samuel Pepys (1633-1703)

Alas! Another instance of the triumph of hope over experience.

Samuel Johnson (1709-1784)
On the remarriage of a widower

Marriage makes an end of many short follies— being one long stupidity.

Friedrich Nietzsche (1844-1900)

Nevertheless, a woman who aspired to anything other than marriage was considered something of an oddity:

A man is in general better pleased when he has a good dinner upon his table than when his wife talks Greek.

Samuel Johnson (1709-1784)

Sir, a woman's preaching is like a dog's walking on his hind legs. It is not done well; but you are surprised to find it done at all.

Samuel Johnson (1709-1784)

I consider that women who are authors, lawyers and politicians are monsters.

Pierre Auguste Renoir (1840-1919)

There are no women composers, never have been and possibly never will be.

Sir Thomas Beecham (1879-1961)

In spite of all this condescension, however, Women's Lib may be said to have arrived:

Twenty million young women rose to their feet with the cry "We will not be dictated to," and promptly became stenographers.

G.K. Chesterton (1874-1936)

and women are determined to have the last word:

Whatever women do they must do twice as well as men to be thought half as good. Luckily, this is not difficult.

Charlotte Whitton (1896-1975)
Former mayor of Ottawa

There is no subject under the sun which has not at some time been the target of derogatory comment.

Not surprisingly, a great deal has been said on the subject of friendship and enmity:

> *My friends! There are no friends.*
>
> Aristotle (384-322 BC)

> *I have no trouble with my enemies. But my goddam friends, White, they are the ones that keep me walking the floor nights.*
>
> Warren G. Harding (1865-1923)
> To William A. White

> *It takes your enemy and your friend, working together, to hurt you to the heart; the one to slander you, and the other to get the news to you.*
>
> Mark Twain (1835-1910)

> *My prayer to God is a very short one: "O Lord, make my enemies ridiculous." God has granted it.*
>
> Voltaire (1694-1778)

> *One should forgive one's enemies, but not before they are hanged.*
>
> Heinrich Heine (1797-1856)

> *I do desire we may be better strangers.*
>
> William Shakespeare (1564-1616)
> *As You Like It*

> *I do not love thee, Doctor Fell,*
> *The reason why I cannot tell;*
> *But this I know, and know full well,*
> *I do not love thee, Doctor Fell.*
>
> Thomas Brown (1663-1704)
> Translation of an epigram of Martial

The telling of untruths has always occasioned a certain amount of displeasure:

> *Lord, Lord, how this world is given to lying!*
>
> William Shakespeare (1564-1616)
> *King Henry IV, First Part*

I said in my haste, All men are liars.

Psalm 116:11

I denounce Mr. Bernard De Voto as a fool and a tedious and egotistical fool, as a liar and a pompous and boresome liar.

Sinclair Lewis (1885-1951)

They have committed false report; moreover, they have spoken untruths; secondarily, they are slanders; sixth and lastly, they have belied a lady; thirdly, they have verified unjust things; and to conclude, they are lying knaves.

William Shakespeare (1564-1616)
Much Ado About Nothing

To the first charge Your Excellency I answer that it is a lie, to the second charge I say that it is a damned lie, and to the third charge that it is a damned infernal lie, and Your Excellency I have no more to say.

Thomas Tremlett
Chief Justice of Newfoundland, replying
to charges of corruption 1811

The world has castigated its wise men:

The more I read him, the less I wonder that they poisoned him.

Thomas Babington Macaulay (1800-1859)
On Socrates

Take from him his sophisms, futilities and incomprehensibilities and what remains? His foggy mind.

Thomas Jefferson (1743-1826)
On Plato

Plato is a bore.

Friedrich Nietzsche (1844-1900)

and, of course, its fools:

Now, the Lord lighten thee! Thou art a great fool.

William Shakespeare (1564-1616)
King Henry IV, Second Part

*We, my Lords, may thank Heaven that we have
something better than our brains to depend on.*

Lord Chesterfield (1694-1773)
To the House of Lords

*They never open their mouths without subtracting
from the sum of human knowledge.*

Thomas Reed (1839-1902)
Speaker of the U.S. House of Representatives
On members of Congress

*They say there's but five upon this isle; we are three
of them; if th' other two be brain'd like us, the state
totters.*

William Shakespeare (1564-1616)
The Tempest

Even the alphabet has come under attack!

Thou whoreson zed! thou unnecessary letter!

William Shakespeare (1564-1616)
King Lear

Man's stomach has always been near his heart, and food
and drink have occasioned a great deal of verbal as well
as physical indigestion. Geoffrey Chaucer was among the
first to warn of the dangers of overeating:

O wombe! O bely! O stynkyng cod,
Fulfilled of dong and of corrupcioun!
At either ende of thee foul is the soun.

Geoffrey Chaucer (1340-1400)

They have digged their grave with their teeth.

Thomas Adams (1612-1653)

Certain vegetables have been considered less than
desirable:

Parsley
Is gharsley.

Ogden Nash (1902-1971)

*Cauliflower is nothing but cabbage with a college
education.*

Mark Twain (1835-1910)

A cucumber should be well sliced, and dressed with pepper and vinegar, and then thrown out, as good for nothing.

Samuel Johnson (1704-1789)

MOTHER: *It's broccoli, dear.*
CHILD: *I say it's spinach, and I say the hell with it.*

E.B. White (b. 1899)
Caption to cartoon by Carl Rose

Boiled cabbage à l'Anglaise *is something compared with which steamed coarse newsprint bought from bankrupt Finnish salvage dealers and heated over smoky oil stoves is an exquisite delicacy. Boiled British cabbage is something lower than ex-Army blankets stolen by dispossessed Goanese dosshousekeepers who used them to cover busted-down hen houses in the slum district of Karachi, found them useless, threw them in anger into the Indus, where they were recovered by convicted beachcombers with grappling irons, who cut them in strips with shears and stewed them in sheep dip before they were sold to dying beggars. Boiled cabbage!*

William Connor (Cassandra) (1909-1967)

Unsatisfactory dinner parties have been the cause of much grief:

This was a good dinner enough, to be sure; but it was not a dinner to ask a man to.

Samuel Johnson (1704-1789)

They make a rare Soop they call Pepper-Pot; its an excellent Breakfast for a Salamander, or a good preparative for a Mountebanks Agent, who Eats Fire one day, that he may get better Victuals the next. Three Spoonfuls so Inflam'd my Mouth, that had I devour'd a Peck of Horse-Radish, and Drank after it a Gallon of Brandy and Gunpowder, I could not have been more importunate for a Drop of Water to cool my Tongue.

Edward Ward (1667-1731)

A particularly bad review was forthcoming if the dinner speaker was poor:

> *I don't know whether Phoebus fled from the dinner table of Thyestes: at any rate, Ligurinus, we fell from yours. Splendid, indeed, it is, and magnificently supplied with good things; but when you recite you spoil it all. I don't want you to set before me a turbot or a two-pound mullet; I don't want your mushrooms or your oysters. I want you to keep your mouth shut!*

Marcus Valerius Martial (c. 40-104 AD)

A preoccupation with appropriate behavior at the dinner table has always been a mark of polite society:

> *Being set at the table, scratch not thyself, and take thou heed as much as thou can'st to spit, cough and to blow at thy nose; but if it be needful, do it dexterously without much noise, turning they face sideling.*

Frances Hawkins
Youth's Behaviour, 1663

An eminent preacher could not understand the fuss about special foods—

> *Why is not a rat as good as a rabbit? Why should men eat shrimps and neglect cockroaches?*

Henry Ward Beecher (1813-1887)

a solution which may have been forced on the composer of this sad little table-grace:

> *Heavenly Father, bless us*
> *And keep us all alive,*
> *There's ten of us to dinner,*
> *And not enough for five.*

Anonymous
Hodge's Grace c.1850

It goes without saying that the imbibing of too much strong drink has always been roundly condemned:

> *Woe to you that are mighty to drink wine, and stout men at drunkenness.*

Isaiah 5:22

Whiskey and vermouth cannot meet as friends, and the Manhattan is an offense against piety.

Bernard De Voto (1897-1956)

A variety of other concoctions has been substituted for whiskey and wine; but none of them, it seems, is without its detractors:

*Cocoa is a cad and coward,
Cocoa is a vulgar beast.*

G.K. Chesterton (1874-1936)

Free yourselves from the slavery of tea and coffee and other slopkettle.

William Cobbett (1762-1835)

Why do they always put mud into coffee on board steamers? Why does the tea generally taste of boiled boots?

William Makepeace Thackeray (1811-1863)

Heaven sent us Soda Water
As a torment for our crimes.

G.K. Chesterton (1874-1936)

The world of the arts provides a fertile vineyard for sour grapes. Those who follow the craft of writing seldom have a good word to say for it:

No one but a blockhead ever wrote, except for money.

Samuel Johnson (1704-1789)

Novels are receipts to make a whore.

Matthew Greene (1696-1737)

but everyone agrees that writers, and indeed all artists, are ruthless in pursuing their work:

If a writer has to rob his mother, he will not hesitate; the "Ode on a Grecian Urn" is worth any number of old ladies.

William Faulkner (1897-1962)

The true artist will let his wife starve, his children go barefoot, his mother drudge for his living at seventy, sooner than work at anything but his art.

Bernard Shaw (1856-1950)

Too often this diligence is not rewarded by the appreciation of others. Musicians, particularly, bear the brunt of constant criticism. The importance of music has often been downgraded:

He knew music was Good, but it didn't sound right.

George Ade (1866-1944)

Hell is full of musical amateurs.
Music is the brandy of the damned.

Bernard Shaw (1856-1950)

> *Perhaps it was because Nero played the fiddle, they burned Rome.*
>
> Oliver Herford (1863-1935)

and some musical instruments frowned upon:

> *He was a fiddler, and consequently a rogue.*
>
> Jonathan Swift (1667-1745)

> *The vile squeaking of his wry-necked fife.*
>
> William Shakespeare (1564-1616)

including the favorite of the Scots:

> *... Others, when the bag-pipe sings i' the nose, Cannot contain their urine.*
>
> William Shakespeare (1564-1616)
The Merchant of Venice

Often musicians themselves have not been held in high esteem. One who endured the jeers and hoots of his contemporaries was the composer Richard Wagner:

> *I like Wagner's music better than any other music. It is so loud that one can talk the whole time without people hearing what one says. That is a great advantage.*
>
> Oscar Wilde (1854-1900)

> *Wagner, thank the fates, is no hypocrite. He says right out what he means, and he usually means something nasty.*
>
> James G. Huneker (1860-1921)

> *Wagner's music is better than it sounds.*
>
> Mark Twain (1835-1910)

> *Wagner has beautiful moments but awful quarter hours.*
>
> Gioacchino Antonio Rossini (1792-1868)

> *Wagner is evidently mad.*
>
> Hector Berlioz (1803-1869)

> *Is Wagner a human being at all? Is he not rather a disease?*
>
> Friedrich Nietzsche (1844-1900)

I love Wagner, but the music I prefer is that of a cat hung up by its tail outside a window and trying to stick to the panes of glass with its claws.

Charles Baudelaire (1821-1867)

Many other musical performances have undergone this kind of critical analysis, including one noteworthy amateur recital:

Miss Truman is a unique American phenomenon with a pleasant voice of little size and fair quality ...yet Miss Truman cannot sing very well. She is flat a good deal of the time ...she communicates almost nothing of the music she presents ...There are few moments during her recital when one can relax and feel confident that she will make her goal, which is the end of the song.

Paul Hume
Music critic of the *Washington Post*
On a recital by Margaret Truman 1950

while modern musical forms have hardly been exempt:

Jazz: *Music invented for the torture of imbeciles.*

Henry van Dyke (1852-1933)

I occasionally play works by contemporary composers and for two reasons. First to discourage the composer from writing any more and secondly to remind myself how much I appreciate Beethoven.

Jascha Heifetz (b. 1901)

Painters, too, suffered a lack of understanding in their audience:

A tortoise-shell cat having a fit in a platter of tomatoes.

Mark Twain (1835-1910)
On a painting by Turner

If the old masters had labeled their fruit, one wouldn't be so likely to mistake pears for turnips.

Mark Twain (1835-1910)

*If my husband would ever meet a woman on the
street who looked like the women in his paintings,
he would fall over in a dead faint.*

Mrs. Pablo Picasso

and a popular cartoonist adopted a cynical view of
current tendencies in painting:

*Abstract art? A product of the untalented, sold by
the unprincipled to the utterly bewildered.*

Al Capp (b. 1909)

A famous modern sculptor attracted restrained admiration from a cranky modern poet:

*Epstein is a great sculptor. I wish he would wash,
but I believe Michael Angelo never did, so I
suppose it is part of the tradition.*

Ezra Pound (1885-1972)

One of the champions of new forms in both art and
writing was the American author, Gertrude Stein, and
her reception was typical of the reaction to the
contemporary arts:

Gertrude Stein is the mama of dada.

*Miss Stein was a past master in making nothing
happen very slowly.*

Clifton Fadiman (b. 1904)

*There's a wonderful family called Stein,
There's Gert and there's Epp and there's Ein;
Gert's poems are bunk,
Epp's statues are junk,
And no one can understand Ein.*

Anonymous

Those whose ambition is to enrich their conversation
with a higher quality of insult and abuse, those who
aspire to the perfect squelch, have a difficult road to
follow. It is comforting to know that we can always turn
for inspiration to the old standby, Shakespeare, who
seems to have a line for every occasion:

Down, down to hell; and say I sent thee thither.

King Henry VI, Third Part

You blocks, you stones, you worse than senseless things!

Julius Caesar

The first thing we do, let's kill all the lawyers.
King Henry VI, Second Part

How now, you secret black and midnight hags! What is't you do?

Macbeth

O villain! thou wilt be condemn'd into everlasting redemption for this.

Much Ado About Nothing

Sweep on, you fat and greasy citizens!
Antony and Cleopatra

William Shakespeare (1546-1616)

It is inspiring, too, to realize that although the art of invective has been in a regrettable decline in recent years, a few hardy souls still keep it alive. Regular perusal of the "Letters" column of most newspapers will reveal anonymous artists at work, and give hope for the future:

Sir: During the short time since The Sun *started publishing in Edmonton, I have witnessed your decay from amiable drunk through voyeur and track rat to misogynous, vitriolic pariah.*

... I cannot but from now on dismiss your scribblings as the libelous drivel of an unbalanced mind.

Robert Hamilton

Edmonton *Sun* 1978

*

The devil damn thee black, thou cream-faced loon!
William Shakespeare (1546-1616)
Macbeth

*

Fatheads! Beanbrains!

Italian proverb

THE UNDISPUTED FAME ENJOYED
BY SHAKESPEARE AS A WRITER ... IS, LIKE
EVERY OTHER LIE,
A GREAT EVIL.

—TOLSTOY

I·WOULD·THE·GODS
HAD·MADE·THEE
MORE·POETICAL·

 *would the gods had made thee more poetical ...*

William Shakespeare (1564-1616)
As You Like It

"Oh, that mine adversary had written a book," lamented Job. Generations of poets, playwrights and novelists since then have learned to their sorrow that the mere act of taking pen to paper leaves a writer open to attack. Literary men and women not only face frontal assault from the critics; they must protect their flanks and rear from the sniping of friends and colleagues. Those who make their living with words seem to be particularly adept at sharpening them as weapons. And perhaps the celebrated artistic temperament is responsible for the remarkably waspish character of a great deal of literary dialogue and the frequency, bitterness and intensity of literary feuds.

Shakespeare has been elevated to a virtually unassailable position among writers of all languages. Yet neither in his own time nor subsequently has the Bard been free from barbs; whether from a green-eyed contemporary —

> *There is an upstart crow beautified with our feathers. That with his tyger's heart wrapt in a player's hide, supposes he is as well able to bombast out a blank verse as the best of you; and being an absolute* Johannes Factotum, *is, in his own conceit, the only Shakescene in a country.*

Robert Greene (1558-1592)

a bored courtier of the Restoration —

> *I saw Hamlet Prince of Denmark, played; but now the old plays begin to disgust this refined age, since his majesty has been so long abroad.*

John Evelyn (1620-1706)

an irreverent monarch —

> *Was there ever such stuff as great part of Shakes-peare? only one must not say so! But what think you — What? Is there not sad stuff? What? — What?*
>
> George III (1738-1820)

or an enraged foreigner:

> *The undisputed fame enjoyed by Shakespeare as a writer ... is, like every other lie, a great evil.*
>
> Count Leo Tolstoy (1828-1910)

The easily pleased Pepys found Shakespeare a bore:

> *To the King's Theatre, where we saw* Midsummer Night's Dream, *which I had never seen before, nor shall ever again, for it is the most insipid, ridiculous play that ever I saw in my life.*
>
> Samuel Pepys (1633-1703)

while a Scottish audience preferred a Scot:

> *Whaur's yer Wully Shakespeare noo?*
>
> Anonymous Scottish theatregoer
> On first night of Scottish play *Douglas* 1756

and the Americans were aghast:

> *Shakespeare, Madam, is obscene, and, thank God, we are sufficiently advanced to have found it out.*
>
> Quoted by Frances Trollope (1780-1863)

But perhaps the most sustained attack on Shakespeare was mounted by one of his own countrymen, a fellow playwright. From a perspective of three centuries, Bernard Shaw took issue with Shakespeare, carrying away a couple of other public monuments in the process:

> *With the single exception of Homer, there is no eminent writer, not even Sir Walter Scott, whom I can despise so entirely as I despise Shakespeare when I measure my mind against his. The intensity of my impatience with him occasionally reaches such a pitch, that it would positively be a relief to me to dig him up and throw stones at him, knowing as I*

do how incapable he and his worshippers are of understanding any less obvious form of indignity.

Bernard Shaw (1856-1950)
On William Shakespeare

This exercise in provocative journalism brought on the return fire of the faithful:

The way Bernard Shaw believes in himself is very refreshing in these atheistic days when so many people believe in no God at all.

Israel Zangwill (1864-1926)

The theatre itself has endured a siege of insults for nearly two thousand years. From the early Church fathers—

Spending time in the theatres produces fornication, intemperance, and every kind of impurity.

St. John Chrysostom (345?-407)

to turbulent nineteenth-century France—

One should never take one's daughter to a theatre. Not only are plays immoral; the house itself is immoral.

Alexandre Dumas *fils* (1824-1895)

to modern musical comedy—

Don't put your daughter on the stage, Mrs. Worthington!

Noel Coward (1899-1973)

the message has always been the same:

That popular Stage-playes ... are sinfull, heathenish, lewde, ungodly Spectacles, and most pernicious Corruptions; condemned in all ages, as intolerable Mischiefes to Churches, to Republickes, to the manners, mindes and soules of men. And that the Profession of Play-poets, of Stageplayers; together with the penning, acting, and frequenting of Stage-playes, are unlawful, infamous and misbeseeming Christians.

William Prynne (1600-1669)

The ire of the early Puritans was particularly violent:

> *I am persuaded that Satan hath not a more speedy way and fitter school to work and teach his desire, to bring men and women into his share of concupiscence and filthy lusts of wicked whoredom, than those plays and theatres . . .*
>
> John Northbrooke

Not every condemnation of the theatre has been based on morality. Later commentators were repelled for different reasons:

> *There is a total extinction of all taste: our authors are vulgar, gross, illiberal; the theatre swarms with wretched translations, and ballad operas, and we have nothing new but improving abuse.*
>
> Horace Walpole (1717-1797)

> *Aside from the moral contamination incident to the average theatre, the influence intellectually is degrading. Its lessons are morbid, distorted, and superficial; they do not mirror life.*
>
> T.T. Munger

> *Is it a stale remark to say that I have constantly found the interest excited at a playhouse to bear an exact inverse proportion to the price paid for admission?*
>
> Charles Lamb (1775-1834)

> *English plays,*
> *Atrocious in content,*
> *Absurd in form,*
> *Objectionable in action,*
> *Execrable English theatre!*
>
> Johann Wolfgang von Goethe (1749-1832)

But a sage of the enlightenment took just the opposite view:

> *Whoever condemns the theatre is an enemy to his country.*
>
> Voltaire (1694-1778)

Poetry, too, has been a ripe field for the caustic critic.

John Milton, the great seventeenth-century poet, met with a certain lack of enthusiasm on literary grounds:

> *Our language sunk under him.*
>
> Joseph Addison (1672-1719)
> On John Milton

> Paradise Lost *is one of the books which the reader admires and lays down, and forgets to take up again. Its perusal is a duty rather than a pleasure.*
>
> Samuel Johnson (1709-1784)

> *This obscure, eccentric and disgusting poem.*
>
> Voltaire (1694-1778)

But it was his political involvement that provoked the lowest blow (the poet had recently lost his sight):

> *Having never had any mental vision, he has now lost his bodily sight; a silly coxcomb, fancifying himself a beauty; an unclean beast, with nothing more human about him than his guttering eyelids; the fittest doom for him would be to hang him on the highest gallows, and set his head on the Tower of London.*
>
> Salmasius (Claude de Saumaise) (1588-1653)
> On John Milton

The late seventeenth century was the age of poetic satire, and many a heroic couplet laid bare the deficiencies of the author's literary rivals. The leading exponent of this sort of verse was the malicious and venomous Alexander Pope, whose tiny stature, low origins and verbal sting earned him the nickname "the wicked wasp of Twickenham":

> *The verses, when they were written, resembled nothing so much as spoonfuls of boiling oil, ladled out by a fiendish monkey at an upstairs window upon such of the passers-by whom the wretch had a grudge against.*
>
> Lytton Strachey (1880-1932)
> On Alexander Pope

Pope's boiling oil scalded a wide variety of victims, most of high estate—

> *Yet let me flap this bug with gilded wings,*
> *This painted child of dirt, that stinks and stings ...*
>> Alexander Pope (1688-1744)
>> On Lord Hervey

> *His passion still, to covet general praise,*
> *His life, to forfeit it a thousand ways.*
>> Alexander Pope (1688-1744)
>> On Lord Wharton

some of low—as in these verses written for the collar of the Prince Regent's pet dog:

> *I am His Highness' dog at Kew;*
> *Pray tell me, sir, whose dog are you?*
>> Alexander Pope (1688-1744)

He clearly relished the deference won by his scathing tongue:

> *Yes, I am proud; and must be proud, to see*
> *Men not afraid of God afraid of me.*
>> Alexander Pope (1688-1744)

—a jibe which gave one of the wounded a chance to get a little of his own back:

> *The great honour of that boast is such*
> *That hornets and mad dogs may boast as much.*
>> Lord Hervey (1696-1743)
>> On Alexander Pope

Prose writers, no less than poets and dramatists, took full part in the literary fray:

> *Now, it must be understood that ink is the great*
> *missive weapon in all battles of the learned, which,*
> *conveyed through a sort of engine called a quill,*
> *infinite numbers of these are darted at the enemy*
> *by the valiant on both sides, with equal skill and*
> *violence, as if it were an engagement of porcupines.*
>> Jonathan Swift (1667-1745)

Swift knew whereof he spoke. Some quills he darted himself:

> *I cannot but conclude the bulk of your natives to be*

> *the most pernicious race of little odious vermin that
> nature ever suffered to crawl upon the surface of the
> earth.*
>
> Jonathan Swift (1667-1745)
> *Gulliver's Travels*

and others were launched in his direction:

> *A monster gibbering shrieks, and gnashing impre-
> cations against mankind — tearing down all shreds
> of modesty, past all sense of manliness and shame;
> filthy in word, filthy in thought, furious, raging,
> obscene.*
>
> William Makepeace Thackeray (1811-1863)
> On Jonathan Swift

The towering literary figure of the late eighteenth century
was Dr. Samuel Johnson — literary critic, compiler of the
famous dictionary, but above all, a brilliant and formidable conversationalist. The age demanded slashing and
often rude repartee, and the gruff, bearlike Johnson was a
master of the verbal put-down — the more because he
knew it was expected of him. Recorded by the omnipres-
ent James Boswell, by Fanny Kemble and Mrs. Thrale,
many of Johnson's sallies retain their vigor even today.

The good doctor had outspoken opinions on many of his contemporaries and on an inexhaustible variety of other subjects:

> *Mrs. Montagu has dropt me. Now Sir, there are people whom one should like very well to drop, but would not wish to be dropt by.*
>
> *
>
> *Sir, I never did the man an injury; yet he would read his tragedy to me.*
>
> *
>
> *Sir, there is no settling the precedency between a louse and a flea.*
>
> On being asked whether Herrick or
Smart was the better poet
>
> *
>
> *Sir, he was dull in company, dull in his closet, dull everywhere. He was dull in a new way, and that made many people think him GREAT. He was a mechanical poet.*
>
> On Thomas Gray
>
> *
>
> *He hardly drank tea without a strategem.*
>
> On Alexander Pope
>
> *Why, Sir, Sherry is dull, naturally dull; but it must have taken him a great deal of pains to become what we now see him. Such excess of stupidity, Sir, is not in nature.*
>
> On Thomas Sheridan
>
> *
>
> *The misfortune of Goldsmith in conversation is this: he goes on without knowing how he is to get off.*
>
> On Oliver Goldsmith
>
> *
>
> *No man will be a sailor who has contrivance enough to get himself into a jail; for being in a ship is being in a jail, with the chance of being drowned. A man in jail has more room, better food, and commonly better company.*
>
> *
>
> PATRON: *n.s. One who countenances, supports or protects. Commonly a wretch who supports with insolence, and is paid with flattery.*
>
> Samuel Johnson (1709-1784)

Not everyone admired Johnson's style —

> *Johnson made the most brutal speeches to living persons; for though he was good-natured at bottom, he was ill-natured at top. He loved to dispute to show his superiority. If his opponents were weak, he told them they were fools; if they vanquished him, he was scurrilous.*
>
> Horace Walpole (1717-1797)

> *Casts of manure a wagon-load around*
> *To raise a simple daisy from the ground;*
> *Uplifts the club of Hercules, for what?*
> *To crush a butterfly or brain a gnat!*
>
> John Wolcot (1738-1819)
On Samuel Johnson

or, for that matter, Boswell's:

> *Have you got Boswell's most absurd enormous book? — the best thing in it is a bon mot of Lord Pembroke. The more one learns of Johnson, the more preposterous assemblage he appears of strong sense, of the lowest bigotry and prejudices, of pride, brutality, fretfulness and vanity — and Boswell is the ape of most of his faults, without a grain of his sense. It is the story of a mountebank and his zany.*
>
> Horace Walpole (1717-1797)

> *Sir, you have but two topics, yourself and me. I am sick of both.*
>
> Samuel Johnson (1709-1784)
To James Boswell

Johnson's definition of a patron may have been tempered by his experience with Lord Chesterfield. He had appealed to Chesterfield for his patronage during the preparation of the Dictionary, but the nobleman made no helpful move until, ten hard years later, when the great work was ready for publication, he wrote two supporting articles. Enraged at Chesterfield's opportunism, Johnson sent him a classical and icy rebuke:

> *Is not a patron, my lord, one who looks with unconcern on a man struggling for life in the water,*

*and when he has reached ground encumbers him
with help? The notice which you have been pleased
to take of my labours, had it been early, had been
kind; but it has been delayed until I am indifferent,
and cannot enjoy it; till I am known, and do not
want it. I hope it is no very cynical asperity not to
confess obligations where no benefit has been
received, or to be unwilling that the public should
consider me as owing that to a patron which
Providence has enabled me to do for myself. Having
carried on my work thus far with so little obligation
to any favourer of learning, I shall not be disap-
pointed though I should conclude it, if less be
possible, with less; for I have been long wakened
from that dream of hope, in which I once boasted
myself with so much exultation, my lord — Your
lordship's most humble, most obedient servant,*
Sam. Johnson

Samuel Johnson (1709-1784)
To Lord Chesterfield

When Chesterfield's letters of advice to his son were
published, Johnson observed:

*They inculcate the morals of a whore, and the
manners of a dancing master.*
Samuel Johnson (1709-1784)

One of the sensations of the day was James MacPherson's "translation" of an obscure Scottish epic poem.
When Johnson denounced "Ossian" as a forgery,
MacPherson challenged him to a duel. The doctor sent a
peremptory reply:

*Mr. James MacPherson — I received your foolish
and impudent letter. Any violence offered me I shall
do my best to repel; and what I cannot do for myself,
the law shall do for me. I hope I shall never be
deterred from detecting what I think to be a cheat,
by the menaces of a ruffian.*

*What would you have me retract? I thought your
book an imposture; I think it an imposture still. For*

*this opinion I have given my reasons to the publick
which I here dare you to refute. Your rage I defy.
Your abilities ... are not so formidable; and what I
hear of your morals, inclines me to pay regard not to
what you shall say, but to what you shall prove. You
may print this if you will.*

Sam. Johnson.

Samuel Johnson (1709-1784)

When Johnson died he was memorialized by his contemporaries in epitaphs that were less than charitable:

*Here lies Sam Johnson: —Reader, have a care,
Tread lightly, lest you wake a sleeping bear:
Religious, moral, generous and humane
He was: but self-sufficient, proud, and vain.
Fond of, and overbearing in, dispute,
A Christian and a scholar — but a brute.*

Soame Jenyns (1704-1787)
On Samuel Johnson

Another superb conversationalist whose life spanned the
eighteenth and nineteenth centuries was the Reverend
Sidney Smith, sometime Canon of St. Paul's Cathedral.
Smith's attitude to the world was one of amused
tolerance. More urbane and less pompous than Johnson,
he used the needle rather than the club:

*No one minds what Jeffrey says. .... It's not more
than a week ago that I heard him speak disrespect-
fully of the Equator.*

*I have to believe in the Apostolic Succession. There
is no other way of explaining the descent of the
Bishop of Exeter from Judas Iscariot.*

*He has spent all his life in letting down empty
buckets into empty wells; and he is frittering away
his age in trying to draw them up again.*

Sidney Smith (1771-1845)

When Lord Brougham, a lawyer with an unsavoury

reputation, arrived at the theatre during a performance of *The Messiah,* Smith announced:

> *Here comes counsel for the other side.*
>
> Sidney Smith (1771-1845)
On Lord Brougham

Smith's droll wit encompassed subjects as diverse as music —

> *Nothing can be more disgusting than Oratorio. How absurd, to see five hundred people fiddling like madmen about the Israelites in the Red Sea!*

country living —

> *I have no relish for the country. It is a kind of healthy grave.*

and the Church —

> *There are three sexes — men, women and clergymen.*
>
> Sidney Smith (1771-1845)

When it was proposed that St. Paul's be surrounded by a wooden sidewalk, Smith agreed:

> *Let the Dean and Canons lay their heads together and the thing will be done.*
>
> Sidney Smith (1771-1845)

Many of his jibes were at his own expense:

> *When I am in the pulpit, I have the pleasure of seeing my audience nod approbation while they sleep.*
> *
> *You and I are exceptions to the laws of nature; you have risen by your gravity, and I have sunk by my levity.*
>
> Sidney Smith (1771-1845)

The ironic Smith tone of voice is at its best in this civilized note to Lord John Russell:

> *You say you are not convinced by my pamphlet. I*

am afraid that I am a very arrogant person, but I do assure you, that in the fondest moments of self-conceit, the idea of convincing a Russell that he was wrong never came across my mind. Euclid would have had a bad chance with you if you had happened to have formed an opinion that the interior angles of a triangle were not equal to two right angles. The more poor Euclid demonstrated, the more you would not have been convinced.

Sydney Smith (1771-1845)
To Lord John Russell

A favorite target of Smith and many others was the brilliant but ponderous Thomas Babington Macaulay. Macaulay was a nonstop talker, and his friends despaired of getting a word in edgewise:

You know, when I am gone you will be sorry you never heard me speak.

Sydney Smith (1771-1845)
To Thomas Babington Macaulay

Macaulay is laying waste society with his water-spouts of talk; people in his company burst for want of an opportunity of dropping in a word.

Henry Reeve
On Thomas Babington Macaulay

Macaulay is well for a while, but one wouldn't live under Niagara.

Thomas Carlyle (1795-1881)
On Thomas Babington Macaulay

Macaulay is like a book in breeches ... he has occasional flashes of silence that make his conversation perfectly delightful.

Sydney Smith (1771-1845)
On Thomas Babington Macaulay

Macaulay read omniverously almost from the time he could walk. He never forgot a thing—

He could repeat the whole History of the Virtuous Blue-Coat Boy in 3 volumes, post 8vo, without a slip.

> *He should take two tablespoonfuls of the waters of*
> *Lethe every morning.*
>
> Sidney Smith (1771-1845)
On Thomas Babington Macaulay

and he was only too prepared to share his awesome knowledge with others:

> *I wish I was as cocksure of anything as Tom*
> *Macaulay is of everything.*
>
> Viscount Melbourne (1770-1848)

> *He not only overflowed with learning, but stood in*
> *the slop.*
>
> Sidney Smith (1771-1845)
On Thomas Babington Macaulay

As an essayist and literary critic, as well as a lawyer, politician and administrator, Macaulay had frequent opportunities to launch thunderbolts of his own:

> *His imagination resembled the wings of an ostrich.*
> *It enabled him to run, though not to soar.*
>
> Thomas Babington Macaulay (1800-1859)

Macaulay took a dim view of British hypocrisy:

> *The Puritan hated bear-baiting, not because it gave*
> *pain to the bear, but because it gave pleasure to the*
> *spectators.*

> *We know no spectacle so ridiculous as the British*
> *public in one of its periodical fits of morality.*
>
> Thomas Babington Macaulay (1800-1859)

He was not a fan of James Boswell, the chronicler of Johnson:

> *Servile and impertinent, shallow and pedantic, a*
> *bigot and a sot, bloated with family pride, and*
> *eternally blustering about the dignity of a born*
> *gentleman, yet stooping to be a talebearer, an*
> *eavesdropper, a common butt in the taverns of*
> *London. ... Everything which another man would*
> *have hidden, everything the publication of which*
> *would have made another man hang himself, was*

matter of exaltation to his weak and diseased mind.
Thomas Babington Macaulay (1800-1859)
On James Boswell

But it was in his review of the memoirs of the French revolutionary, Bertrand Barère, that Macaulay achieved what has been described, with only slight exaggeration, as "the most sustained piece of invective in the English language."

> *. . . Our opinion then is this: that Barère approached nearer than any person mentioned in history or fiction, whether man or devil, to the idea of consummate and universal depravity. In him the qualities which are the proper objects of contempt, preserve an exquisite and absolute harmony. When we put everything together, sensuality, poltroonery, baseness, effrontery, mendacity, barbarity, the result is something which in a novel we should condemn as caricature, and to which, we venture to say, no parallel can be found in history.*

> *. . . A man who has never been within the tropics does not know what a thunderstorm means; a man who has never looked on Niagara has but a faint idea of a cataract; and he who has not read Barère's* Memoirs *may be said not to know what it is to lie.*
Thomas Babington Macaulay (1800-1859)
On Bertrand Barère

For all Macaulay's ability, there were those who did not think much of him:

> *At bottom, this Macaulay is but a poor creature with his dictionary literature and erudition, his saloon arrogance. He has no vision in him. He will neither see nor do any great thing.*
Thomas Carlyle (1795-1881)
On Thomas Babington Macaulay

The power of the press was beginning to make itself felt, and personal attack was the vogue. The anonymous letters of "Junius" appeared in the popular *Public*

Advertiser, and one of them disembowelled the descendant of an illegitimate son of Charles II:

> *It is not that you do wrong by design, but that you should never do right by mistake. It is not that your indolence and your activity have been equally misapplied, but that the first uniform principle or ... genius of your life, should have carried you through every possible change and contradiction of conduct without the momentary imputation or colour of a virtue; and that the wildest spirit of inconsistency should never once have betrayed you into a wise or honourable action ...*
>
> *You may look back with pleasure to an illustrious pedigree in which heraldry has not left a single good quality upon record to insult or upbraid you. ... Charles the First lived and died a hypocrite. Charles the Second was a hypocrite of another sort, and should have died upon the same scaffold. At the distance of a century, we see their different characters happily revived, and blended in your Grace. Sullen and severe without religion, profligate without gaiety, you live like Charles the Second, without being an amiable companion, and, for aught I know, may die as his father did, without the reputation of a martyr.*

"Junius"
Letter to the Duke of Grafton 1769

The early nineteenth century saw the dawn of the Romantic Age, and it brought a series of fierce literary skirmishes. The Romantic poets were a wild and prickly group, viewed by many as barbarians. When they were not firing back at their critics, they trained their sights on one another.

The consumptive John Keats was the first conspicuous victim. His lush verses were, it seems, little appreciated by at least one of his fellow poets:

> *Here are Jonny Keats' piss-a-bed poetry, and three novels by God knows whom. ... No more Keats, I*

entreat: flay him alive; if some of you don't I must skin him myself: there is no bearing the drivelling idiotism of the Mankin.

Lord Byron (1788-1824)

Keats's work was savagely attacked by the fashionable literary magazines, the *Quarterly Review* and *Blackwood's*:

The Phrenzy of the "Poems" was bad enough in its way; but it did not alarm us half so seriously as the calm, settled, imperturbable drivelling idiocy of "Endymion." ... Mr. Hunt is a small poet, but he is a clever man. Mr. Keats is a still smaller poet, and he is only a boy of pretty abilities, which he has done everything in his power to spoil ... We venture to make one small prophecy, that his bookseller will not a second time venture £50 upon any thing he can write. It is a better and a wiser thing to be a starved apothecary than a starved poet; so back to the shop, Mr. John, back to "plasters, pills, and ointment boxes," etc.

Blackwood's Magazine
On John Keats 1818

JOHN KEATS

Keats promptly died, and his friend and champion Shelley promoted the notion that he had been mortally wounded by his bad reviews:

> *It may be well said that these wretched men know not what they do. .... What gnat did they strain at here, after having swallowed all those camels? Against what women taken in adultery dares the foremost of these literary prostitutes to cast his opprobrious stone? Miserable man! You, one of the meanest, have wantonly defaced one of the noblest specimens of the workmanship of God. Nor shall it be your excuse that, murderer as you are, you have spoken daggers, but used none.*

Percy Bysshe Shelley (1792-1822)
Preface to "Adonais"

Even Byron had a partial change of heart and weighed in against the critics:

> *Who killed John Keats?*
> *"I", says the Quarterly,*
> *So savage and Tartarly;*
> *"'Twas one of my feats."*

Lord Byron (1788-1824)

But the class-conscious reviewers were unrepentant and their opinion was later shared by Thomas Carlyle, surveying a biography of Keats:

> *Fricassee of dead dog. .... A truly unwise little book. The kind of man that Keats was gets ever more horrible to me. Force of hunger for pleasure of every kind, and want of all other force — such a soul, it would once have been very evident, was a chosen "vessel of Hell".*

Thomas Carlyle (1795-1881)
On Monckton Milnes's *Life of Keats*

Shelley, of course, had good reason to resent the literary reviews. The *Quarterly* had been particularly unkind to him:

> *Mr. Shelley is a very vain man; and like most vain*

> *men, he is but half instructed in knowledge and less than half disciplined in reasoning powers; his vanity ... has been his ruin.*
>
> Quarterly Review
> On Percy Bysshe Shelley 1817

But then, so had some of his fellows:

> *Shelley is a poor creature, who has said or done nothing worth a serious man being at the trouble of remembering. ... Poor soul, he has always seemed to me an extremely weak creature; a poor, thin, spasmodic, hectic shrill and pallid being. ... The very voice of him, shrill, shrieky, to my ear has too much of the ghost.*
>
> Thomas Carlyle (1795-1881)
> On Percy Bysshe Shelley

> *He was a liar and a cheat; he paid no regard to truth, nor to any kind of moral obligation.*
>
> Robert Southey (1774-1843)
> On Percy Bysshe Shelley

> *A lewd vegetarian.*
>
> Charles Kingsley (1819-1875)
> On Percy Bysshe Shelley

Byron's spectacular social life led many to take a skeptical view of him:

> *The most affected of sensualists and the most pretentious of profligates.*
>
> Algernon Swinburne (1837-1909)
> On Lord Byron

> *A denaturalized being who, having exhausted every species of sensual gratification, and drained the cup of sin to its bitterest dregs, is resolved to show that he is no longer human, even in his frailties, but a cool, unconcerned fiend.*
>
> John Styles
> On Lord Byron

but he retaliated with a sharp pen. He did not, it appears, think highly of many of his peers:

*I have no patience with the sort of trash you send me
out by way of books ... I never saw such work or
works. Campbell is lecturing — Moore idling —
Southey twaddling — Wordsworth drivelling —
Coleridge muddling — Joanna Baillie piddling —
Bowles quibbling, squabbling, and snivelling.*

Lord Byron (1788-1824)

*Let simple Wordsworth chime his childish verse,
And brother Coleridge lull the babe at nurse.*

Lord Byron (1788-1824)

Byron didn't mind stooping to attack; he once serenaded
an unfortunately named poet laureate:

*Oh, Amos Cottle — Phoebus, what a name
To fill the speaking trump of future fame!
Oh, Amos Cottle, for a moment think
What meagre profits spring from pen and ink!*

Lord Byron (1788-1824)

Like many of the other Romantics, Byron died young; had
he lived, we might never have heard his name:

*Byron! — he would be all forgotten today if he had
lived to be a florid old gentleman with iron-grey
whiskers, writing very long, very able letters to The
Times about the Repeal of the Corn Laws.*

Max Beerbohm (1872-1956)

One poetic young Turk who did achieve Establishment respectability was William Wordsworth, reaching dubious heights as poet laureate.

> *In his youth, Wordsworth sympathized with the French Revolution, went to France, wrote good poetry, and had a natural daughter. At this period, he was a "bad" man.*
>
> *Then he became "good", abandoned his daughter, adopted correct principles, and wrote bad poetry.*
>
> Bertrand Russell (1872-1970)

> *Just for a handful of silver he left us,*
> *Just for a riband to stick in his coat.*
>
> Robert Browning (1812-1889)
> *The Lost Leader*

It was partly Wordsworth's poetry that upset his critics—

> *Dank, limber verses, stuft with lakeside sedges,*
> *And propt with rotten stakes from rotten hedges.*
>
> Walter Savage Landor (1775-1864)

> *Two voices are there: one is of the deep;*
> *It learns the storm-cloud's thunderous melody ...*
> *And one is of an old half-witted sheep*
> *Which bleats articulate monotony ...*
> *And, Wordsworth, both are thine.*
>
> James Kenneth Stephen (1859-1892)

> *Is Wordsworth a bell with a wooden tongue?*
>
> Ralph Waldo Emerson (1803-1882)

> *Who both by precept and example shows*
> *That prose is verse, and verse is merely prose.*
>
> Lord Byron (1788-1824)

and partly his personality—

> *Wordsworth has left a bad impression wherever he visited in town by his egotism, vanity and bigotry.*
>
> John Keats (1795-1821)

> *For prolixity, thinness, endless dilution, it excels all
> the other speech I had heard from mortals. . . . The
> languid way in which he gives you a handful of
> numb unresponsive fingers is very significant.*
>
> Thomas Carlyle (1795-1881)
On William Wordsworth

The moral repression of the nineteenth century seems
only to have egged on the outspoken; literary infighting
took place in the foothills as well as on the mountain
peaks.

The essayist William Hazlitt also wrote for the
Edinburgh Review, so he was on both sides of the
author-critic controversy. His friends took mild exception to his critiques:

> *In God's name, why could you not tell Mr. Shelley
> in a pleasant manner of what you dislike in him?
> . . . How do you think that friends can eternally
> live upon their good behaviour in this way, and be
> cordial and comfortable or whatever else you
> choose they should be—for it is difficult to find
> out—on pain of being drawn and quartered in
> your paragraphs.*
>
> Leigh Hunt (1784-1859)
To William Hazlitt

while other observers were more forthright:

> *He abuses all poets, with the single exception of
> Milton; he abuses all country-people; he abuses the
> English; he abuses the Irish; he abuses the Scotch.
> . . . if the creature . . . must make his way over the
> tombs of illustrious men, disfiguring the records of
> their greatness with the slime and filth which
> marks his track, it is right to point him out, that he
> may be flung back to the situation in which nature
> designed that he should grovel.*
>
> *Quarterly Review*
On William Hazlitt 1817

> *A mere ulcer; a sore from head to foot; a poor devil*

> *so completely flayed that there is not a square inch*
> *of healthy flesh on his carcass; an overgrown pim-*
> *ple, sore to the touch.*
>
> *Quarterly Review*
> On William Hazlitt 1817

Celebrated persons even considered him socially unacceptable:

> *His manners are 99 in a 100 singularly repulsive.*
> Samuel Taylor Coleridge (1772-1834)

and took their revenge by writing unpleasant little epitaphs:

> *Under this stone does William Hazlitt lie*
> *Thankless of all that God or man could give,*
> *He lived like one who never thought to die,*
> *He died like one who dared not hope to live.*
> Samuel Taylor Coleridge (1772-1834)

The growing savagery of the literary critics provoked the Gaelic wrath of even so amiable a poet as Robert Burns:

> *Thou eunuch of language ... thou pimp of gender*
> *... murderous accoucheur of infant learning*
> *... thou pickle-herring in the puppet show of*
> *nonsense.*
>
> Robert Burns (1759-1796)
> On an anonymous critic

If this seems excessive, it was merely the latest volley in a long war. A sixteenth-century Frenchman expressed the views of authors of all ages:

> *As for you, little envious Prigs, snarling, bastard,*
> *puny Criticks, you'll soon have railed your last: Go*
> *hang yourselves.*
>
> François Rabelais (c. 1490-1553)

In his wake followed a host of others:

> *They who write ill, and they who ne'er durst write,*
> *Turn critics out of mere revenge and spite.*
> John Dryden (1631-1700)

The critic's symbol should be the tumble-bug; he

deposits his egg in somebody else's dung, otherwise he could not hatch it.

Mark Twain (1835-1910)

A louse in the locks of literature.

Alfred, Lord Tennyson (1809-1894)
On critic Churton Collins

and many successors, including angry fathers, have kept the tradition alive:

I have just read your lousy review buried in the back pages. You sound like a frustrated old man who never made a success, an eight-ulcer man on a four-ulcer job, and all four ulcers working. I have never met you, but if I do you'll need a new nose and plenty of beefsteak and perhaps a supporter below.

Harry S Truman (1884-1972)
To *Washington Post* music critic Paul Hume

The verbal jousting of the Romantics merely set the stage for what was to follow. The writers of the later nineteenth century displayed an extraordinary ingenuity in personal abuse.

Leading the field as a one-man demolition squad was the cantankerous Thomas Carlyle, who, afflicted by chronic dyspepsia, suffered fools not gladly and his fellow writers hardly at all:

Charles Lamb I sincerely believe to be in some considerable degree insane. A more pitiful, rickety, gasping, staggering, stammering Tomfool I do not know.

On Charles Lamb

A weak, diffusive, weltering, ineffectual man. ... Never did I see such apparatus got ready for thinking, and so little thought. He mounts scaffolding, pulleys and tackle, gathers all the tools in the neighbourhood with labour, with noise, demonstration, precept, abuse, and sets — three bricks.

On Coleridge

Gladstone appears to me one of the contemptiblest

men I ever looked on. A poor Ritualist; almost spectral kind of phantasm of a man ...

On William Ewart Gladstone

The most unending ass in Christendom.

On Herbert Spencer

I have no patience whatever with these gorilla damnifications of humanity.

On Charles Darwin

Thomas Carlyle (1795-1881)

Carlyle once refused to receive the poet Swinburne, on the grounds that he had no wish to meet someone who was

sitting in a sewer, and adding to it.

In Swinburne, Carlyle met his match, for if anyone could be more vitriolic than the Scot it was this effete young man caricatured as the "fleshly poet" in Gilbert and Sullivan's *Patience*. Swinburne deplored

the immaculate Calvinism of so fiery and so forcible a champion of slave-holding and slave-torture as Mr. Carlyle.

Algernon Swinburne (1837-1909)

and extended the compliment to the rest of the family —

> *That very sorry pair of phenomena, Thomas Cloacina and his Goody.*
>
> Algernon Swinburne (1837-1909)
On the Carlyles

a sentiment shared by others:

> *It was very good of God to let Carlyle and Mrs. Carlyle marry one another and so make only two people miserable instead of four.*
>
> Samuel Butler (1835-1902)

His own poetry was under sustained attack for its supposed immorality (*Punch* called him *"Swine*-born"):

> *I attempt to describe Mr. Swinburne; and lo! the Bacchanal screams, the sterile Dolores sweats, serpents dance, men and women wrench, wriggle, and foam in an endless alliteration of heated and meaningless words ...*
>
> Robert Buchanan (1841-1901)
On Algernon Swinburne

But Swinburne was himself enraged by what he saw as a lack of morality in others. The American poet, Walt Whitman, especially offended him:

> *Under the dirty clumsy paws of a harper whose plectrum is a muck-rake, any tune will become a chaos of dischords. ... Mr. Whitman's Eve is a drunken apple-woman, indecently sprawling in the slush and garbage of the gutter amid the rotten refuse of her overturned fruit-stall: but Mr. Whitman's Venus is a Hottentot wench under the influence of cantharides and adulterated rum.*
>
> Algernon Swinburne (1837-1909)
On Walt Whitman

and even the good grey Tennyson was suspect:

> *The Vivien of Mr. Tennyson's idyll seems to me ... about the most base and repulsive person ever set forth in serious literature. Her impurity is actually eclipsed by her incredible and incomparable vulgar-*

> *ity. . . . She is such a sordid creature as plucks men passing by the sleeve. . . . The conversation of Vivien is exactly described in the poet's own phrase — it is "as the poached filth that floods the middle street."*
>
> Algernon Swinburne (1837-1909)
On Alfred, Lord Tennyson

(Tennyson, on reading his poem *Lucretius* to a friend, was said to remark:

> *What a mess little Swinburne would have made of this.)*

One of Swinburne's most famous run-ins was with the "Sage of Concord," Ralph Waldo Emerson. He had read in an American paper that Emerson had described him as

> *a perfect leper, and a mere sodomite.*

and had promptly dispatched a polite commentary:

> *I am informed that certain American journalists, not content with providing filth of their own for the consumption of their kind, sometimes offer to their readers a dish of beastliness which they profess to have gathered from under the chairs of more distinguished men.*
>
> *I . . . am not sufficiently expert in the dialect of the cesspool and the dung-cart to retort in their own kind on these venerable gentlemen — I, whose ears and lips alike are unused to the amenities of conversation embroidered with such fragments of flowery rhetoric as may be fished up by congenial fingers or lapped up by congenial tongues out of the sewage of Sodom. . . .*
>
> *[These are] the last tricks of tongue now possible to a gap-toothed and hoary-headed ape, . . . who now in his dotage spits and chatters from a dirtier perch of his own finding and fouling . . .*
>
> Algernon Swinburne (1837-1909)
To Ralph Waldo Emerson

The pained Emerson made no reply. Swinburne fired off
another letter, in much the same terms; but the
correspondence did not flourish—perhaps because

> *Emerson is one who lives instinctively on
> ambrosia—and leaves everything indigestible on
> his plate.*
>
> Friedrich Nietzsche (1844-1900)
On Ralph Waldo Emerson

> *I could readily see in Emerson ...a gaping flaw. It
> was the insinuation that had he lived in those days
> when the world was made, he might have offered
> some valuable suggestions.*
>
> Herman Melville (1819-1891)
On Ralph Waldo Emerson

The general reaction to modern literature was summed
up by one disapproving onlooker:

> *Great literature is the creation, for the most part, of
> disreputable characters, many of whom looked
> rather seedy, some of whom were drunken black-
> guards, a few of whom were swindlers or perpetual
> borrowers, rowdies, gamblers or slaves to a drug.*
>
> Alexander Harvey

That Charles Dickens, then at the height of his powers
as a writer, had a good ear for the language of invective
is clear from many satirical passages in his novels—
particularly *The Pickwick Papers*. Occasionally he
employed this talent in earnest:

> *In the foreground of the carpenter's shop is a hid-
> eous, wry-necked, blubbering, red-haired boy in
> a nightgown, who appears to have received a poke
> playing in an adjacent gutter, and to be hold-
> ing it up for the contemplation of a kneeling wo-
> man, so horrible in her ugliness that (supposing it
> were possible for any human creature to exist for a*

*moment with that dislocated throat) she would
stand out from the rest of the company as a monster
in the vilest cabaret in France or the lowest gin-shop
in England.*

Charles Dickens (1812-1870)
On Millais's "Christ in the House of His Parents"

Another figure around whom controversy swirled was
James McNeill Whistler, the expatriate American artist
and notable dandy, who was a champion of the new "art
for art's sake" painters and writers. One of the first to
tangle with Whistler was John Ruskin, the fiercely
moralistic essayist and art critic:

> *Ruskin is one of the most turbid and fallacious
> minds ... of the century. To the service of the most
> wildly eccentric thoughts he brings the acerbity of a
> bigot. ... His mental temperament is that of the
> first Spanish Grand Inquisitor. He is a Torquemada
> of aesthetics. ... He would burn alive the critic who
> disagrees with him. ... Since stakes do not stand
> within his reach, he can at least rave and rage in
> word, and annihilate the heretic figuratively by
> abuse and cursing.*

Max Nordau (1849-1923)
On John Ruskin

Ruskin had little use for the painting of his day,
especially that of the new school:

> *I never saw anything so impudent on the walls of
> any exhibition, in any country, as last year in
> London. It was a daub professing to be a "harmony
> in pink and white" (or some such nonsense);
> absolute rubbish, and which had taken about a
> quarter of an hour to scrawl or daub — it had no
> pretence to be called painting. The price asked for it
> was two hundred and fifty guineas.*

John Ruskin (1819-1900)
On Whistler's "Symphony in Grey and Green"

Offended by Whistler's exotic life-style and "frivolous"
painting, Ruskin continued to belabor him:

I have seen and heard much of cockney impudence before now; but never expected to hear a coxcomb ask two hundred guineas for flinging a pot of paint in the public's face.

John Ruskin (1819-1900)
On Whistler's "The Falling Rocket"

The thin-skinned Whistler promptly sued Ruskin for libel; he won his case, but the jury, art critics themselves no doubt, would award him only a farthing in damages!

An early disciple of Whistler was Oscar Wilde, then building his reputation as a conversational lion.

WILDE: (after a bright remark by Whistler) I wish I had said that!
WHISTLER: You will, Oscar, you will!

Whistler (with good reason) accused Wilde of plagiarism, and the ensuing skirmish was conducted, to universal amusement, in the editorial pages of the London papers:

Sir: What has Oscar in common with Art? except that he dines at our tables and picks from our platters the plums for the pudding he peddles in the provinces. Oscar — the amiable, irresponsible, esurient Oscar — with no more sense of a picture than the fit of a coat, has the courage of the opinions ... of others!

James McNeill Whistler (1834-1903)
The World 1886

Sir: ... As Mr. James Whistler has had the impertinence to attack me with both venom and vulgarity in your columns, I hope you will allow me to state that the assertions contained in his letters are as deliberately untrue as they are deliberately offensive.

As for borrowing Mr. Whistler's ideas about art, the only thoroughly original ideas I have ever heard him express have had reference to his own superiority as a painter over painters greater than himself.

Oscar Wilde (1854-1900)
Truth 1890

OSCAR FINGAL
O'FLAHERTIE WILLS
WILDE c. 1882
IN AMERICA

1978

Whistler finally withdrew from the fray:

> *I'm lonesome. They are all dying. I have hardly a warm personal enemy left.*
>
> James McNeill Whistler (1834-1903)

The polished, sophisticated conversation of Oscar Wilde raised the put-down to a different level. As the nineteenth century drew to a close, his huge success marked a significant change in direction for literary insult. Gradually it has become more detached, less filled with personal venom. Epigrammatic and cynical, Wilde's verbal thrusts were a wry commentary on life, but were basically too good-natured to qualify as invective. He relied heavily on turning the expectations of his listeners upside-down:

> *He is old enough to know worse.*
>
> *
>
> *One of those characteristic British faces that, once seen, are never remembered.*
>
> *
>
> *A cynic is a man who knows the price of everything and the value of nothing.*
>
> *
>
> *The English public takes no interest in a work of art until it is told that the work in question is immoral.*
>
> Oscar Wilde (1854-1900)

Wilde's quips were often personal, but were contrived more for their effect on the audience than on the victim:

> *Henry James writes fiction as if it were a painful duty.*
>
> *
>
> *The gods have bestowed on Max the gift of perpetual old age.*
>
> On Max Beerbohm
>
> *
>
> *George Moore wrote brilliant English until he discovered grammar.*
>
> *
>
> *There are two ways of disliking poetry: one way is to dislike it, the other is to read Pope.*
>
> *
>
> *Bernard Shaw is an excellent man; he has not an enemy in the world, and none of his friends like him.*

The first rule for a young playwright to follow is not to write like Henry Arthur Jones. ... The second and third rules are the same.

Oscar Wilde (1854-1900)

Frank Harris was to become Wilde's biographer:

Frank Harris is invited to all the great houses in England — once.
*
Every great man nowadays has his disciples, and it is always Judas who writes the biography.

Oscar Wilde (1854-1900)

Although he was constantly embroiled in it, Wilde shrank from controversy:

I dislike arguments of any kind. They are always vulgar, and often convincing.

Nor did he admire the literary lions of the day:

One must have a heart of stone to read the death of little Nell without laughing.

On Dickens's *Old Curiosity Shop*

Even at his lowest moment Wilde was able to muster a *bon mot*. Handcuffed, standing in a pouring rain on his way to prison, Oscar remarked:

If this is the way Queen Victoria treats her convicts, she doesn't deserve to have any.

Oscar Wilde (1854-1900)

Meanwhile, across the Atlantic, another brilliant writer and sardonic observer of the human condition was delighting audiences with his wry wit.

He could charm an audience an hour on a stretch without ever getting rid of an idea.

Mark Twain (1835-1910)

Mark Twain was a genuinely funny man, but a vein of pessimism was never far beneath the surface. His lectures were laced with quips and comments that reflected unfavorably on his fellow man.

When some men discharge an obligation, you can hear the report for miles around.

*

I am not an editor of a newspaper and shall always try to do right and be good so that God will not make me one.

*

Man is the only animal that blushes. Or needs to.

*

Such is the human race. Often it does seem a pity that Noah and his party didn't miss the boat.

Mark Twain (1835-1910)

He tended to take a dim view of officialdom in all its guises:

Fleas can be taught nearly anything that a Congressman can.

*

It could probably be shown by facts and figures that there is no distinctively native American criminal class except Congress.

*

In the first place God made idiots; this was for practice; then he made school boards.

Mark Twain (1835-1910)

His admiration for one of the great Empire-builders was not unmixed:

> *I admire him, I frankly confess it; and when his time comes I shall buy a piece of the rope for a keepsake.*
>
> Mark Twain (1835-1910)
> On Cecil Rhodes

Mark Twain had an easily roused temper, and he carried on his campaign against bureaucracy into his private life:

> *Some day you will move me almost to the verge of irritation by your chuckle-headed Goddamned fashion of shutting your Goddamned gas off without giving any notice to your Goddamned parishioners. Several times you have come within an ace of smothering half of this household in their beds and blowing up the other half by this idiotic, not to say criminal, custom of yours. And it has happened again today. Haven't you a telephone?*
>
> Mark Twain (1835-1910)
> Letter to the Gas Company

Yet his sense of humor was irrepressible; the spirit of the man is demonstrated in the joke he played on his close friend, William Howells:

> *To the Editor: I would like to know what kind of goddamn govment this is that discriminates between two common carriers and makes a goddam railroad charge everybody equal and lets a goddam man charge any goddam price he wants to for his goddam opera box.*
>
> *W.D. HOWELLS*

> *Howells, it is an outrage the way the govment is acting so I sent this complaint to N.Y. Times with your name signed because it would have more weight.*
>
> *MARK*
>
> Mark Twain (1835-1910)

A thorn in the side of the complacent for more than half a

century was the Irish-born playwright and critic-at-large, Bernard Shaw. Shaw's views on just about everything set Establishment teeth on edge:

> He's a man of great common sense and good taste—meaning thereby a man without originality or moral courage.
> *
> When a stupid man is doing something he is ashamed of, he always declares that it is his duty.
> *
> It is dangerous to be sincere unless you are also stupid.
> *
> Do not do unto others as you would that they should do unto you. Their tastes may not be the same.
>
> Bernard Shaw (1856-1950)

Shaw was an early champion of the plays of Henrik Ibsen; the new, realistic drama was at first universally rejected by the critics:

> A crazy fanatic ... a crazy cranky being ... not only consistently dirty but deplorably dull.
> *
> A wave of human folly.
> *
> A gloomy sort of ghoul ... blinking like a stupid old owl.
>
> Newspaper reviews of Ibsen's
> *Ghosts* and *Hedda Gabler* 1891

Many of Shaw's own plays received an equally nasty welcome:

> Superabundance of foulness ... wholly immoral and degenerate ... you cannot have a clean pig stye.
> *
> Smells to high heaven. It is a dramatized stench.
>
> Newspaper reviews of Shaw's
> *Mrs. Warren's Profession* 1905

This was a form of rough justice, for Shaw himself did not hesitate to criticize other writers. He was fastidious about the smallest details of how his own work was presented:

> A more horrible offense against Art than what you have put ... on the cover of the Essays, has never

been perpetrated even in Newcastle. I reject your handbill with disdain, with rage, with contumelious epithets. ... Of the hellish ugliness of the block of letterpress headed "What the Press says", I cannot trust myself to write, lest I be betrayed into intemperance of language ... Some time ago you mentioned something about changing the cover ... This is to give you formal notice that if you do anything of the sort ... I will have your heart's blood.

Bernard Shaw (1856-1950)
Letter to his publisher

Shaw's self-satisfaction and self-appointed status as a gadfly invoked the wrath of a wide assortment of detractors:

An Irish smut-dealer.

Anthony Comstock (1844-1915)

An idiot child screaming in a hospital.

H.G. Wells (1866-1946)
On Bernard Shaw

George Bernard Shaw, most poisonous of all the poisonous haters of England; despiser, distorter and denier of the plain truths whereby men live; topsyturvey perverter of all human relationships; menace to ordered social thought and ordered social life; irresponsible braggart, blaring self-trumpeter; idol of opaque intellectuals and thwarted females; calculus of contrariwise; flippertygibbet pope of chaos; portent and epitome of this generation's moral and spiritual disorder.

Henry Arthur Jones (1851-1929)

A dessicated bourgeois ... a fossilized chauvinist, a self-satisfied Englishman ...

Pravda
On Bernard Shaw 1924

But Shaw could outdo them all. In a memorable diatribe, he denounced a bacteriologist, Dr. Edward Bach, who feared the implantation of vicious ape qualities in humans as a result of "monkey-gland" treatments. Shaw's opinion of the human race is never clearer:

> *Has any ape ever torn the glands from a living man to graft them upon another ape for the sake of a brief and unnatural extension of that ape's life? Was Torquemada an ape? Were the Inquisition and the Star Chamber monkey-houses? ... Has it been necessary to found a Society for the Protection of Ape Children, as it has been for the protection of human children? Was the late war a war of apes or of men? Was poison gas a simian or a human invention? How can Dr. Bach mention the word cruelty in the presence of an ape without blushing? ... Man remains what he has always been; the cruelest of all the animals, and the most elaborately and fiendishly sensual.*

Bernard Shaw (1856-1950)

As the twentieth century progressed, the decline of old-fashioned abuse became more apparent. The passionate literary feuds were gone, to be replaced by a more detached, objective — if sometimes equally vicious — form of criticism.

There were exceptions, of course. The inbred world of the universities continued to spawn cutthroat literary in-fighting. A prime example was A.E. Housman. When he was not writing the barefoot poetry of "A Shropshire

Lad," Housman was a noted classical scholar, whose scalpel could neatly filet those whose work was not up to his standards:

> The virtues of his work are quenched and smothered by the multitude and monstrosity of its vices. They say that he was born of human parentage; but if so he must have been suckled by Caucasian tigers. . . .
>
> Not only has Jacob no sense for grammar, no sense for coherency, no sense for sense, but being himself possessed by a passion for the clumsy and the hispid he imputed this disgusting taste to all the authors whom he edited.
>
> A.E. Housman (1859-1936)
> On Friedrich Jacob
>
> Stoeber's mind, though that is no name to call it by . . . turns as unswervingly to the false, the meaningless, the unmetrical, as the needle to the pole.
>
> A.E. Housman (1859-1936)
> On Elias Stoeber

One holdover from the old school was the critic Edmund Gosse, who struggled to maintain the proper standards of literature:

> My attention has just been called to the current no. of The Sphere, where Mr. Clement Shorter, in terms of unexampled insolence, speaks of me as "the so-called critic", and attacks me on the score of an article which he has not seen.
>
> Will you explain to me why I have suddenly received over my head and shoulders this bucket-full of Mr. Clement Shorter's bedroom slops? Can it be that he supposes me to be the author of some attack on him?
>
> If so, pray reassure him. I never attack him, for I never mention him.
>
> Edmund Gosse (1849-1928)
> To Thomas Wise
>
> What does pain me exceedingly is that you should

*write so badly. These verses are execrable, and I am
shocked that you seem unable to perceive it.*

Edmund Gosse (1849-1928)
To Robert Nichols

Gosse was particularly outraged by the publication of
James Joyce's monumental *Ulysses*. As far as he could
understand it, he disapproved of it:

*I have difficulty in describing ... the character of
Mr. Joyce's morality. ... he is a literary charlatan
of the extremest order. His principal book,* Ulysses
*... is an anarchical production, infamous in taste,
in style, in everything. ... He is a sort of M. de Sade,
but does not write so well.*

Edmund Gosse (1849-1928)
On James Joyce

So did almost everyone else —

*The work of a queasy undergraduate scratching his
pimples.*

Virginia Woolf (1882-1941)
On James Joyce

*It is written by a man with a diseased mind and soul
so black that he would even obscure the darkness of
hell.*

Senator Reed Smoot
On James Joyce

including, surprisingly, D.H. Lawrence, who found the
work immoral:

*The last part of it is the dirtiest, most indecent, most
obscene thing ever written. Yes it is, Frieda ... it is
filthy.*
*
My God, what a clumsy olla putrida *James Joyce
is! Nothing but old fags and cabbage-stumps of
quotations from the Bible and the rest, stewed in the
juice of deliberate, journalistic dirty-mindedness.*

D.H. Lawrence (1885-1930)
On James Joyce

Lawrence, himself the recipient of many accusations of obscenity, was not made more charitable by criticism. He had a truly nasty tongue, and he scattered his largesse indiscriminately:

> *I loathe you. You revolt me stewing in your consumption. ... The Italians were quite right to have nothing to do with you.*
>
> D.H. Lawrence (1885-1930)
> To Katherine Mansfield

> *Spit on her for me when you see her, she's a liar out and out. As for him, I reserve my language. ... Vermin, the pair of 'em.*
>
> D.H. Lawrence (1885-1930)
> On Katherine Mansfield and J. Middleton Murray

> Never *adapt yourself. Kick Brill in the guts if he tries to come it over you. Kick all America in the guts: they need it. ... Spit on every neurotic, and wipe your feet on his face if he tries to drag you down to him. ... All that "arty" and "literary" crew, I know them, they are smoking, steaming shits.*
>
> D.H. Lawrence (1885-1930)
> To Mabel Dodge Luhan

Occasionally a note of humor crept in, as in his comment on a damning review of his paintings by T.W. Earp:

> *I heard a little chicken chirp:*
> *My name is Thomas, Thomas Earp,*
> *and I can neither paint nor write,*
> *I can only put other people right.*
>
> D.H. Lawrence (1885-1930)

But Lawrence's characteristic attitude was one of rage against all the dolts who would not appreciate him:

> *Curse the blasted, jelly-boned swines, the slimy, the belly-wriggling invertebrates, the miserable sodding rotters, the flaming sods, the snivelling, dribbling, dithering, palsied, pulseless lot that make up England today. They've got white of egg in their veins, and their spunk is that watery it's a marvel they can breed. They* can *nothing but* frog-spawn — *the gibberers! God, how I hate them!*
>
> D.H. Lawrence (1885-1930)

This type of vitriol was now the exception. The new writers and critics were in the Oscar Wilde tradition, skewering their victims with witty and sophisticated phrases. The moving spirits were the scintillating group whose headquarters was the Round Table of the Algonquin Hotel in New York, and the zenith of this art form was reached in the drama reviews of the 1930s (although there are earlier examples):

> Hook and Ladder *is the sort of play that gives failures a bad name.*
>
> Walter Kerr (b. 1913)

> *He played the King as though under momentary apprehension that someone else was about to play the ace.*
>
> Eugene Field (1850-1895)
> On actor Creston Clarke's performance as King Lear

> *Tallulah Bankhead barged down the Nile last night as Cleopatra — and sank.*
>
> John Mason Brown (b. 1900)

Very well then: I say Never.
George Jean Nathan (1882-1958)
On *Tonight or Never*

It was one of those plays in which all the actors unfortunately enunciated very clearly.
Robert Benchley (1889-1945)

He has delusions of adequacy.
Walter Kerr (b. 1913)
On an anonymous actor

The scenery was beautiful but the actors got in front of it. The play left a taste of lukewarm parsnip juice.
Alexander Woollcott (1887-1943)

Katherine Hepburn ran the whole gamut of emotions from A to B.
Dorothy Parker (1893-1967)

The brightest star in this firmament was Dorothy Parker—brittle, perceptive, salty, endowed with fast reflexes and an acid wit:

A combination of Little Nell and Lady Macbeth.
Alexander Woollcott (1887-1943)
On Dorothy Parker

Her reviews of books and plays reflect these qualities:

The affair between Margot Asquith and Margot Asquith will live as one of the prettiest love stories in all literature.
On a four-volume autobiography
*
This is not a novel to be tossed aside lightly. It should be thrown with great force.
*
Tonstant Weader fwowed up.
On *The House at Pooh Corner*
In her column "Constant Reader"

Dorothy Parker was also adept at a pointed pun—as when, at a Hallowe'en party, she remarked:

Ducking for apples—change one letter and it's the story of my life.
Dorothy Parker (1893-1967)

The eccentric style of Gertrude Stein provoked a devastating parody-cum-rejection slip from her editor:

> *I am only one, only one, only one. Only one being, one at the same time. Not two, not three, only one. Only one life to live, only sixty minutes in one hour. Only one pair of eyes. Only one brain. Only one being. Being only one, having only one pair of eyes, having only one time, having only one life, I cannot read your MS three or four times. Not even one time. Only one look, only one look is enough. Hardly one copy would sell here. Hardly one. Hardly one.*

A.J. Fifield
To Gertrude Stein

H.L. Mencken was a provocative newspaper columnist whose irreverence inevitably attracted retaliation. Mencken gleefully published a sampler of the abuse hurled at him.

> *With a pig's eyes that never look up, with a pig's snout that loves muck, with a pig's brain that knows only the sty, and a pig's squeal that cries only when he is hurt, he sometimes opens his pig's mouth, tusked and ugly, and lets out the voice of God, railing at the whitewash that covers the manure about his habitat.*

William Allen White (1868-1944)
On H.L. Mencken

> *Mr. Mencken talks about truth as if she were his mistress, but he handles her like an iceman.*

Stuart P. Sherman
On H.L. Mencken

> *Mencken, with his filthy verbal hemorrhages, is so low down in the moral scale, so damnably dirty, so vile and degenerate, that when his time comes to die it will take a special dispensation from Heaven to get him into the bottommost pit of Hell.*

Jackson News
On H.L. Mencken

The present literary scene is relatively calm, but there will always be writers who enjoy hurling verbal brickbats for their own sake. And as long as there is a reading public, literary controversy will not die. Witness this recent flurry in the correspondence columns of the *Manchester Guardian,* between an angry middle-aged playwright and a gaggle of poison-pens:

Sir: Having recently seen St. Joan *in London and* Caesar and Cleopatra *in Sydney, it is clearer to me than ever that Shaw is the most fraudulent, inept writer of Victorian melodramas ever to gull a timid critic or fool a dull public.*

He writes like a Pakistani who has learned English when he was twelve years old in order to become a chartered accountant.

John Osborne
*
Sir: What's wrong with Mr. Osborne shows clearly in what he says about Shaw: Mr. Osborne has no wit about him, and thus he never sees anything as complex or funny.

And another thing: Shaw would never have been guilty of such a racial slur as Mr. Osborne offhandedly committed. Shaw was a good and brilliant man. ... Had he created Mr. Osborne, he would have relieved his heavy dullness with something lovable.

(Prof.) Bert G. Hornback
*
Sir: I suggest that Shaw will be remembered with respect when no one looks back in anger — or any other emotion — at the rabid rantings and pompous twaddle of John Osborne.

Michael Crawford
Manchester Guardian 1977
*
Get stewed: books are a load of crap.

Philip Larkin (b. 1922)

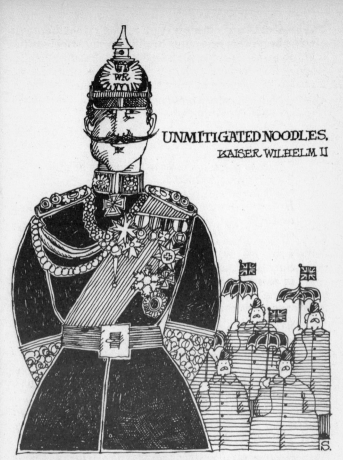

UNMITIGATED NOODLES.
KAISER WILHELM II

THE·LAND·GOD GAVE·TO·CAIN·

I am rather inclined to believe that this is the land God gave to Cain.

Jacques Cartier (1491-1557)
On Labrador

Breathes there the man with soul so dead,
Who never to himself hath said
"This is mine own, my native land"?

Sir Walter Scott (1771-1832)

Probably not. And one of the offshoots of strong national pride is the tendency to exalt one's own country by denigrating others. Every country in the world has been derided by the citizens of other lands, pained or outraged that the object of their scorn does not measure up to their own high standards. Tourists and emigrants are particularly prone to contrast the people and customs they meet on their journeys with those wonderful ones they left home to escape.

No nation on earth has suffered more slings and arrows than England. Nearly two thousand years of relationships with other peoples have ensured this. The English have found disfavor with the Romans, the French, the Spanish, the Dutch, the Germans and, more recently, the Americans — and in not a few cases, the feeling has mounted to a passionate hatred.

Poltroons, cowards, skulkers and dastards.

Eustache Deschamps (fourteenth century)

England, the heart of a rabbit in the body of a lion,
The jaws of a serpent, in an abode of popinjays.

Eugene Deschamps (fourteenth century)

The perfidious, haughty, savage, disdainful, stupid,
slothful, inhospitable, inhuman English.

Julius Caesar Scaliger (1540-1609)

Paralytic sycophants, effete betrayers of humanity, carrion-eating servile imitators, arch-cowards and collaborators, gang of women-murderers, degenerate rabble, parasitic traditionalists, play-boy soldiers, conceited dandies.

Approved terms of abuse for East German Communist speakers when describing Britain 1953

Unmitigated noodles.

Kaiser Wilhelm II of Germany (1859-1941)

The earliest tourists were warned of the dangers of British travel:

You must look out in Britain that you are not cheated by the charioteers.

Marcus Tullius Cicero (106-43 BC)

and subsequent commentators agreed that the English were crooked:

In all the four corners of the earth one of these three names is given to him who steals from his neighbour: brigand, robber or Englishman.

Les Triades de l'Anglais 1572

A pirate spreading misery and ruin over the face of the ocean.

Thomas Jefferson (1743-1826)

The most common epithet through the years has been that of "perfidious Albion":

The English are, in my opinion, perfidious and cunning, plotting the destruction of the lives of foreigners, so that even if they humbly bend the knee, they cannot be trusted.

Leo de Rozmital 1456

I know why the sun never sets on the British Empire: God wouldn't trust an Englishman in the dark.

Duncan Spaeth

The defects of the national character are apparently without number. Englishmen are none too bright —

The English are, I think the most obtuse and barbarous people in the world.

Stendhal (Marie Henri Beyle) (1783-1842)

An Englishman will burn his bed to catch a flea.

Turkish proverb

they are indolent —

> *... They are naturally lazy, and spend half their time in taking Tobacco.*
>
> Samuel de Sorbière (1615-1670)

It is related of an Englishman that he hanged himself to avoid the daily task of dressing and undressing.

Johann Wolfgang von Goethe (1749-1832)

unreliable —

> *The English have no exalted sentiments. They can all be bought.*
>
> Napoleon Bonaparte (1769-1821)

puritanical —

> *A nation of ants, morose, frigid, and still preserving the same dread of happiness and joy as in the days of John Knox.*
>
> Max O'Rell (Paul Blouet) 1883

taciturn —

> *Silence: a conversation with an Englishman.*
>
> Heinrich Heine (1797-1856)

inartistic —

> *The English are not a sculptural nation.*
>
> N. Pevsner 1955

These people have no ear, either for rhythm or music, and their unnatural passion for pianoforte playing and singing is thus all the more repulsive. There is nothing on earth more terrible than English music, except English painting.

Heinrich Heine (1797-1856)

hypocritical —

> *What a pity it is that we have no amusements in England but vice and religion!*
>
> Sidney Smith (1771-1845)

and dull —

> *From every Englishman emanates a kind of gas, the deadly choke-damp of boredom.*
>
> Heinrich Heine (1797-1856)

There were those who maintained that the English were not quite as bad as they seemed:

> *I think that those who accuse the English of being cruel, envious, distrustful, vindictive and libertine, are wrong. It is true that they take pleasure in seeing gladiators fight, in seeing bulls torn to pieces by dogs, seeing cocks fight, and that in the carnivals they use batons against the cocks, but it is not out of cruelty so much as coarseness.*
>
> G.L. LeSage 1715

It was difficult to expect anything better of these God-forsaken people, considering the language they had to speak:

> *To learn English you must begin by thrusting the jaw forward, almost clenching the teeth, and practically immobilizing the lips. In this way the English produce the series of unpleasant little mews of which their language consists.*
>
> José Ortega y Gasset (1883-1955)

> *The devil take these people and their language! They take a dozen monosyllabic words in their jaws, chew them, crunch them and spit them out again, and call that speaking. Fortunately they are by nature fairly silent, and although they gaze at us open-mouthed, they spare us long conversations.*
>
> Heinrich Heine (1797-1856)

But most observers seemed agreed that the unfortunate

qualities of the English could be attributed to two factors: their weather —

> *It is cowardly to commit suicide. The English often kill themselves — it is a malady caused by the humid climate.*
>
> Napoleon Bonaparte (1769-1821)

> *The way to endure summer in England is to have it framed and glazed in a comfortable room.*
>
> Horace Walpole (1717-1797)

> *On a fine day the climate of England is like looking up a chimney; on a foul day, like looking down one.*
>
> Anonymous

and their food. English tastes and English cookery have always astonished an unbelieving world:

> *Go back, you dissolute English,*
> *Drink your beer and eat your pickled beef.*
>
> *La Repentance des Anglais et des Espagnols* 1522

The English, who eat their meat red and bloody, show the savagery that goes with such food.

J.O. de la Mettrie (1709-1751)

There are in England sixty different religious sects and only one sauce.

Caracciolo (d. 1641)

More recent travellers have continued to be disenchanted by the level of English cuisine:

The average cooking in the average hotel for the average Englishman explains to a large extent the English bleakness and taciturnity. Nobody can beam and warble while chewing pressed beef smeared with diabolical mustard. Nobody can exult aloud while ungluing from his teeth a quivering tapioca pudding.

Karel Čapek (1890-1938)

Such fare, of course, produced inevitable results:

Belching at table, and in all companies whatsoever, is a thing which the English no more scruple than they do coughing and sneezing.

H. Misson de Valbourg 1698

Can there be anything left to criticize? Yes — English clothing:

Englishwomen's shoes look as if they had been made by someone who had often heard shoes described, but had never seen any.

Margaret Halsey 1938

cold English houses:

An Englishman absolutely believes that he can warm a room by building a grate-fire at the end of it.

Stephen Fiske 1869

and even the very windows:

English windows open only half-way, either the top half or the bottom half. One may even have the pleasure of opening them a little at the top and a

*little at the bottom, but not at all in the middle. The
sun cannot enter openly, nor the air. The window
keeps its selfish and perfidious character. I hate the
English windows.*

Sarah Bernhardt (1844-1896)

That vast and pulsing metropolis, London, horrified
some onlookers with its contrasts:

London! Dirty little pool of life.

B.M. Malabari (b. 1893)

*London, black as crows and as noisy as ducks,
prudish with all the vices in evidence, everlast-
ingly drunk, in spite of ridiculous laws about
drunkenness, immense, though it is really basically
only a collection of scandal-mongering boroughs,
vying with each other, ugly and dull, without any
monuments except interminable docks.*

Paul Verlaine (1844-1896)

The ultimately unforgivable sin of the English, in the
eyes of others, is their infuriating attitude of calm
superiority to the rest of the world:

*In the eyes of the Englishman the Frenchman is a
dog, the Spaniard a fool, the German a drunkard,
the Italian a bandit. . . . Only the Englishman is the*
non plus ultra *of perfection, and Nature's master-
piece.*

A. Riem 1798-9

*The ordinary Britisher imagines that God is an
Englishman.*

Bernard Shaw (1856-1950)

*

Scotland and Ireland have been the butt of many jokes —
chiefly, it must be admitted, at the hands of their fellow
islanders, the English.

*I have been trying all my life to like Scotchmen, and
am obligated to desist from the experiment in
despair.*

Charles Lamb (1775-1834)

It requires a surgical operation to get a joke well into a Scotch understanding.

Sidney Smith (1771-1845)

DR. JOHNSON: *Sir, it is a very vile country.*
MR. S——: *Well, Sir, God made it.*
DR. JOHNSON: *Certainly he did, but we must remember that He made it for Scotchmen; and comparisons are odious, Mr. S——, but God made Hell.*

Samuel Johnson (1709-1784)

Much may be made of a Scotchman, if he be caught young.

Samuel Johnson (1709-1784)

Sir, ... the noblest prospect which a Scotchman ever sees, is the high road that leads him to England!

Samuel Johnson (1709-1784)

There are few more impressive sights in the world than a Scotsman on the make.

James M. Barrie (1860-1937)

He is the fine gentleman whose father toils with a muck-fork. ... He is the bandy-legged lout from Tullietudlescleugh, who, after a childhood of intimacy with the cesspool and the crablouse, and twelve months at "the college" on moneys wrung from the diet of his family, drops his threadbare kilt and comes south in a slop suit to instruct the English in the arts of civilisation and in the English language.

T.W.H. Crosland (1865-1924)
The Unspeakable Scot

*
The Irish are a fair people; they never speak well of one another.

Samuel Johnson (1709-1784)

A servile race in folly nursed,
Who truckle most when treated worse.

Jonathan Swift (1667-1745)

If one could only teach the English how to talk and

the Irish how to listen, society would be quite civilized.

Oscar Wilde (1854-1900)

Give an Irishman lager for a month, and he's a dead man. An Irishman is lined with copper, and the beer corrodes it. But whiskey polishes the copper and is the saving of him.

Mark Twain (1835-1910)

Put an Irishman on the spit, and you can always get another Irishman to turn him.

Bernard Shaw (1856-1950)

*

Surprisingly enough, very few bad things have been said about the United States. Nothing like the immense body of vituperation against England exists. America came of age as a world power only in the mid-twentieth century — at a period when creative invective was almost dead — and as a result has escaped much of the true nastiness older nations have endured.

This is not to say that everyone has always spoken well of America. A constant flow of overseas visitors has come, seen and been unimpressed with American manners and customs. Their condescension and patronizing attitude infuriated Americans — and not the least when the things they said were true!

Knavery seems to be so much the striking feature of its inhabitants that it may not in the end be an evil that they will become aliens to this country.

George III of England (1738-1820)

I am willing to love all mankind, except an American.

Samuel Johnson (1709-1784)

A nineteenth-century traveler was amazed at the extreme manifestations of American social "delicacy:"

On being ushered into the reception room, conceive my astonishment at beholding a square piano-forte with four limbs. So that the ladies who visited ...

> *might feel in its full force the extreme delicacy of the*
> *mistress of the establishment ... she had dressed*
> *all these four limbs in modest little trousers, with*
> *frills at the bottom of them!*
>
> Frederick Marryat (1792-1848)

while another was horrified by the less attractive aspects
of good old American hustle:

> *There is constant activity going on in one small*
> *portion of the brain; all the rest is stagnant. The*
> *money-making faculty is alone cultivated. They are*
> *incapable of acquiring general knowledge on a*
> *broad or liberal scale. All is confined to trade,*
> *finance, law, and small, local provincial informa-*
> *tion. Art, science, literature, are nearly dead letters*
> *to them.*
>
> T.C. Grattan (1792-1864)

English visitors, accustomed to the mouldy dampness of
their own houses, constantly complained about central
heating:

> *The method of heating many of the best houses is a*
> *terrible grievance to persons not accustomed to it,*
> *and a fatal misfortune to those who are. Casual*
> *visitors are nearly suffocated, and constant occupi-*
> *ers killed. An enormous furnace in the cellar sends*
> *up, day and night, streams of hot air, through*
> *apertures and pipes, to every room in the house. ...*
> *It meets you the moment the street-door is opened to*
> *let you in, and rushes after you when you emerge*
> *again, half-stewed and parboiled, into the whole-*
> *some air. The self-victimized citizens, who have a*
> *preposterous affection for this atmosphere, un-*
> *doubtedly shorten their lives by it. Several elderly*
> *gentlemen of my acquaintance, suddenly cut off,*
> *would assuredly have had a verdict of "died of a*
> *furnace" pronounced on their cases, had a coroner*
> *been called.*
>
> T.C. Grattan (1792-1864)

Self-appointed gourmets found the culinary scene a
disaster:

> ... *Every broken-down barber, or disappointed dancing-master, French, German or Italian, sets up as cook with about as much knowledge of cookery as a cow has of cowcumbers. In a word, the science of the table is at the earliest stage of infancy in the United States.*
>
> T.C. Grattan (1792-1864)

One apparently universal custom met with revulsion from visitors:

> *I hardly know any annoyance so deeply repugnant to English feelings, as the incessant remorseless spitting of Americans.*
>
> Frances Trollope (1780-1863)

> *America is one long expectoration.*
>
> Oscar Wilde (1854-1900)

> *You never can conceive what the hawking and spitting is, the whole night through. Last night was the worst. Upon my honour and word I was obliged, this morning, to lay my fur-coat on the deck, and wipe the half-dried flakes of spittle from it with my handkerchief: and the only surprise seemed to be, that I should consider it necessary to do so. When I turned in last night, I put it on a stool beside me, and there it lay, under a cross-fire from five men — three opposite; one above; and one below. I make no complaints and show no disgust.*
>
> Charles Dickens (1812-1870)

On the whole, Dickens was not favorably impressed with Americans:

> *Their demeanor ... is invariably morose, sullen, clownish, and repulsive. I should think there is not, on the face of the earth, a people so entirely destitute of humour, vivacity, or the capacity of enjoyment.*
>
> Charles Dickens (1812-1870)

Without doubt the critic who upset the Americans most was Frances Trollope, mother of the famous novelist Anthony Trollope. Returning to England after four years' residence in America in the 1820s, her commentary on American life and manners became a *cause célèbre* in both England and the United States. Travelling on a Mississippi steamer, the fastidious Mrs. Trollope was dismayed by American lack of couth:

> *The total want of all the usual courtesies of the table, the voracious rapidity with which the viands were seized and devoured; the strange uncouth phrases and pronunciation; the loathsome spitting, from the contamination of which it was absolutely impossible to protect our dresses; the frightful manner of feeding with their knives, till the whole blade seemed to enter into the mouth; and the still more frightful manner of cleaning the teeth afterwards with a pocket-knife, soon forced us to feel that we were not surrounded by the generals, colonels and majors of the old world; and that the dinner-hour was to be anything rather than an hour of enjoyment.*

Frances Trollope (1780-1863)

Mrs. Trollope found the natives stingy —

> *I suppose there is less alms-giving in America than in any other Christian country on the face of the globe. It is not in the temper of the people either to give or to receive.*

Frances Trollope (1780-1863)

white-faced —

> *The ladies have strange ways of adding to their charms. They powder themselves immoderately, face, neck, and arms, with pulverised starch; the effect is indescribably disagreeable by day-light, and not very favourable at any time.*

Frances Trollope (1780-1863)

and stooped —

> *I never saw an American man walk or stand well; ... they are nearly all hollow chested and round shouldered.*

Frances Trollope (1780-1863)

Above all she was repelled by what she felt was gross commercialism:

> *I heard an Englishman, who had been long resident in America, declare that in following, in meeting, or in overtaking, in the street, on the road, or in the field, at the theatre, the coffee-house, or at home, he had never overheard Americans conversing without the word* DOLLAR *being pronounced between them. Such unity of purpose ... can ... be found nowhere else, except ... in an ant's nest.*
>
> Frances Trollope (1780-1863)

Mrs. Trollope, you will be glad to hear, loved the scenery!

ANTHONY TROLLOPE C. 1855

Later travellers were less scathing but still found much to criticize. Mrs. Trollope's son did not have a good time in New York:

> *Speaking of New York as a traveller I have two faults to find with it. In the first place there is nothing to see; and in the second place there is no mode of getting about to see anything.*
>
> Anthony Trollope (1815-1882)

while another budding young writer was patronizing:

> *The American has no language. He has dialect, slang, provincialism, accent, and so forth.*
>
> Rudyard Kipling (1865-1936)

Always there was the recurring complaint about American hot air:

> *Alas, you are parboiled by a diabolic chevaux-de-frise of steam pipes which refuse to be turned off, and insist on accompanying your troubled slumbers by an intermittent series of bubbles, squeaks and hisses.*
>
> James F. Muirhead

The author of *Vanity Fair* found no improvement in American table-manners:

> *The European continent swarms with your people. They are not all as polished as Chesterfield. I wish some of them spoke French a little better. I saw five of them at supper at Basle the other night with their knives down their throats. It was awful.*
>
> William Makepeace Thackeray (1811-1863)

By this time the foreign critics had been joined by the home-grown; henceforth it was to be a mixed chorus:

> *The Americans, like the English, probably make love worse than any other race.*
>
> Walt Whitman (1819-1892)

> *"The American Nation in the Sixth Ward is a fine people," he says. "They love th' eagle," he says, "on the back iv a dollar."*
>
> Finley Peter Dunne (1867-1936)
> *Mr. Dooley*

> *Of course, America had often been discovered before Columbus, but it had always been hushed up.*
>
> Oscar Wilde (1854-1900)

> *America is the only nation in history which miraculously has gone directly from barbarism to degeneration without the usual interval of civilization.*
>
> Georges Clemenceau (1841-1929)

> *It is absurd to say that there are neither ruins nor*

curiosities in America when they have their mothers and their manners.

Oscar Wilde (1854-1900)

The 100% American is 99% an idiot.

Bernard Shaw (1856-1950)

When you become used to never being alone, you may consider yourself Americanized.

André Maurois (1885-1967)

American women expect to find in their husbands the perfection that English women only hope to find in their butlers.

W. Somerset Maugham (1874-1965)

The trouble with America is that there are far too many wide open spaces surrounded by teeth.

Charles Luckman

Don't get the idea that I'm one of these goddam radicals. Don't get the idea that I'm knocking the American system.

Al Capone (1899-1947)

You are right in your impression that a number of persons are urging me to come to the United States.

But why on earth do you call them my friends?

Bernard Shaw (1856-1950)

The thing that impresses me most about America is the way parents obey their children.

The Duke of Windsor (1894-1972)

No one ever went broke underestimating the taste of the American public.

H.L. Mencken (1880-1956)

Regionalism thrives in the United States, and some states and cities attract criticism as honey does flies. Texas is a favorite target:

If I owned Texas and Hell, I would rent out Texas and live in Hell.

General Philip H. Sheridan (1831-1888)

and so is big, bad New York:

If there ever was an aviary overstocked with jays it is that Yaptown-on-the-Hudson called New York.

O. Henry (1862-1910)

New York — A city of 7,000,000 so decadent that when I leave it I never dare look back lest I turn into

salt and the conductor throw me over his left shoulder for good luck.

Frank Sullivan

Prim, correct Boston has its eccentricities:

Boston is a moral and intellectual nursery always busy applying first principles to trifles.

George Santayana (1863-1952)

while Chicago has occasionally been compared to another warm spot:

Here is the difference between Dante, Milton, and me. They wrote about hell and never saw the place. I wrote about Chicago after looking the town over for years and years.

Carl Sandburg (1878-1967)

The new western mecca is a universal source of fun:

California is a fine place to live in — if you happen to be an orange.

Fred Allen

His great aim was to escape from civilization, and, as soon as he had money, he went to Southern California.

Anonymous

along with its most notorious community:

Hollywood is a sewer with service from the Ritz Carlton.

Wilson Mizner

They know only one word of more than one syllable here, and that is fillum.

Louis Sherwin
On Hollywood

Perhaps Mark Twain summed up what many observers still feel about the United States:

It was wonderful to find America, but it would have been more wonderful to miss it.

Mark Twain (1835-1910)

Mme de Pompadour

Canada, a country with a relatively small population and no pretentions to power, has not attracted cataracts of outside criticism; those who noticed her at all tended to dismiss her:

> *You know that these two nations are at war for a few acres of snow, and that they are spending ... more than all Canada is worth.*
>
> Voltaire (1694-1778)

> *It makes little difference; Canada is useful only to provide me with furs.*
>
> Madame de Pompadour (1721-1764)
On the fall of Quebec

> *I fear that I have not got much to say about Canada, not having seen much; what I got by going to Canada was a cold.*
>
> Henry David Thoreau (1817-1862)

> *I don't even know what street Canada is on.*
>
> Al Capone (1899-1947)

while those who probed a little deeper found a depressing stagnation:

Canada is a country without a soul ... live, but not like the States, kicking.

Rupert Brooke (1887-1915)

As false as a diamond from Canada.

Popular French saying, after 1542

Feller Citizens, this country is goin' to the dogs hand over hand.

T.C. Haliburton (1795-1861)
Sam Slick

For many years Canadians accepted their lack of consequence humbly, and rather self-righteously made a virtue of it:

> *There are too many nasty little self-centred nations in the world already; God forbid that Canada should add one to the number!*

W.L. Grant (1872-1935)

They have been wont to define themselves in deprecating terms:

> *A Canadian is somebody who knows how to make love in a canoe.*

Pierre Berton 1973

> *A Canadian is someone who drinks Brazilian coffee from an English teacup, and munches a French pastry while sitting on his Danish furniture, having just come home from an Italian movie in his German car. He picks up his Japanese pen and writes to his Member of Parliament to complain about the American takeover of the Canadian publishing business.*

Campbell Hughes 1973

The Canadian imagination has always been dominated by the climate:

> *This gloomy region, where the year is divided into one day and one night, lies entirely outside the stream of history.*

W.W. Reade 1872

> *Canada has a climate nine months' winter and three months late in the fall.*
>
> American saying (late nineteenth century)

Canada's first novelist did not find the weather an incentive in her work:

> *I no longer wonder the elegant arts are unknown here; the rigour of the climate suspends the very powers of the understanding: what then must become of those of the imagination? ... Genius will never mount high, where the faculties of the mind are benumbed half the year.*
>
> Frances Brooke (1745-1789)

The absence of the elegant arts and the general philistinism of Canadians were bemoaned by foreigners and native-born alike:

> *The cold narrow minds, the confined ideas, the bygone prejudices of the society are hardly conceivable; books there are none, nor music, and as to pictures! — the Lord deliver us from such! The people do not know what a picture is.*
>
> Anna Jameson (1794-1860)

> *The only poet in Canada was very nice to me in Ottawa. Canada's a bloody place for a sensitive real poet like this to live all his life in.*
>
> Rupert Brooke (1887-1915)

> *Tonight I give lecture to Art Students' League. I want a picture of a horse to show that animal is beautiful because every part made for function, without ornament. In Paris I would show woman, but in Toronto I show a horse.*
>
> Anonymous French artist 1931

An early poet struck a note of frustration —

> *How utterly destitute of all light and charm are the intellectual conditions of our people and the institutions of our public life! How barren! How barbarous!*
>
> Archibald Lampman (1861-1899)

but a popular comedian has supplied a solution:

> *Support your fellow Canadians. We should buy lousy Canadian novels instead of importing lousy American novels.*
>
> Johnny Wayne 1968

The precarious co-existence between English and French in Canada has provided a stimulating national sport:

> *That the two tribes of men, French and English, do not assimilate is no new discovery; it is nothing more than Nature herself did when she deliberately created the British Channel.*
>
> Sir Francis Bond Head (1793-1875)

> *English was good enough for Jesus Christ.*
>
> Ralph Melnyk
> On bilingualism

> *All pro athletes are bilingual. They speak English and profanity.*
>
> Gordie Howe 1975

Like the United States, Canada is a country of regions, and each province has its own special charms:

I find that Newfoundland is said to be celebrated for its codfish, its dogs, its hogs, its fogs!

Sir William Whiteway (1828-1908)
Former Prime Minister of Newfoundland

The purity of the air of Newfoundland is without doubt due to the fact that the people of the outports never open their windows.

J.G. Millais 1907

A rascally heap of sand, rock and swamp, called Prince Edward Island, in the horrible Gulf of St. Lawrence; that lump of worthlessness ... bears nothing but potatoes ...

William Cobbett (1762-1835)

Good God, what sums the nursing of that ill-throven, hardvisaged and ill-favoured brat, Nova Scotia, has cost to this wittol nation.

Edmund Burke (1729-1797)

Quebec does not have opinions — only sentiments.

Sir Wilfrid Laurier (1841-1919)

Quebec is not a province like the others. She is a little more stupid.

Gérard Filion 1963

Let the Eastern bastards freeze in the dark!

Alberta bumper sticker 1973

British Columbia is a barren, cold, mountain country that is not worth keeping. ... the place has been going from bad to worse. Fifty railroads would not galvanise it into prosperity.

Henry Labouchère (1798-1869)

A number of Canadian cities have endeared themselves to the nation — Halifax:

We have upwards of one hundred licensed houses and perhaps as many more ... without license; so that the business of one half of the town is to sell rum and the other half to drink it.

Anonymous 1760

Montreal:

> *O God! O Montreal!*
>
> Samuel Butler (1835-1902)
> *A Psalm of Montreal*

> *Montreal is the only place where a good French accent isn't a social asset.*
>
> Brendan Behan (1923-1964)

Ottawa, the capital:

> *A sub-arctic lumber village converted by royal mandate into a political cock-pit.*
>
> Goldwin Smith (1823-1910)

Kingston:

> *Indeed, it may be said of Kingston, that one-half appears to be burnt down, and the other half not to be built up.*
>
> Charles Dickens (1812-1870)

Winnipeg:

> *So this is Winnipeg; I can tell it's not Paris.*
>
> Bob Edwards (1864-1922)

Medicine Hat:

> *You people in this district seem to have all Hell for a basement.*
>
> Rudyard Kipling (1865-1936)

and of course, Toronto. Hating Toronto is the second national sport:

> *The situation of the town is very unhealthy, for it stands on a piece of low marshy land, which is better calculated for a frog-pond or beaver meadow than for the residence of human beings.*
>
> Edward Talbot (1801-1839)

> *Houses of ill-fame in Toronto? Certainly not. The whole city is an immense house of ill-fame.*
>
> C.S. Clark (1826-1909)

> *Toronto as a city carries out the idea of Canada as a*

> *country. It is a calculated crime both against the aspirations of the soul and the affection of the heart.*
>
> Aleister Crowley 1906

Even that scenic wonder, Niagara Falls, has found carping critics:

> *Niagara Falls is simply a vast unnecessary amount of water going the wrong way and then falling over unnecessary rocks.*
>
> Oscar Wilde (1854-1900)

> *When I first saw the falls I was disappointed in the outline. Every American bride is taken there, and the sight must be one of the earliest, if not the keenest, disappointments of American married life.*
>
> Oscar Wilde (1854-1900)

*

Hardly a country on earth has escaped having its tenderest patriotic feelings trampled. The French have been assailed for some well-known national qualities:

> *France was long a despotism tempered by epigrams.*
>
> Thomas Carlyle (1795-1881)

> *Your nation is divided into two species: the one of idle monkeys who mock at everything; and the other of tigers who tear.*
>
> Voltaire (1694-1778)

> *How can one conceive of a one-party system in a country that has over two hundred varieties of cheeses?*
>
> Charles de Gaulle (1890-1970)

while the Germans have attracted solemn observations:

> *The German mind has a talent for making no mistakes but the very greatest.*
>
> Clifton Fadiman (b. 1904)

> *One thing I will say for the Germans, they are always perfectly willing to give somebody else's land to somebody else.*
>
> Will Rogers (1879-1935)

> *Life is too short to learn German.*
>
> Richard Porson (1759-1808)

The Chinese are inscrutable:

> *There are only two kinds of Chinese — those who give bribes and those who take them.*
>
> Russian proverb

the Greeks wily:

> *Greeks tell the truth, but only once a year.*
>
> Russian proverb

> *After shaking hands with a Greek, count your fingers.*
>
> Albanian proverb

and the Russians enigmatic:

> *Russia — a riddle wrapped in a mystery inside an enigma.*
>
> Winston Churchill (1874-1965)

> *Make ye no truce with Adam-zad — the bear that walks like a man.*
>
> Rudyard Kipling (1865-1936)

*

Comparisons are odious, but probably inevitable:

> *Canada could have enjoyed:*
> *English government,*
> *French culture,*
> *and American know-how.*

> *Instead it ended up with:*
> *English know-how,*
> *French government,*
> *and American culture.*
>
> John Robert Colombo 1965

*

The final choice, of course, is between two countries from which no traveler returns:

> *Heaven for climate; Hell for society.*
>
> Mark Twain (1835-1910)

TALKING·OF·THE·BADNESS
OF·THE·GOVERNMENT·

alking of the badness of the Government, where nothing but wickedness, and wicked men and women command the king ...

Samuel Pepys (1633-1703)

Pepys was in good company, for "talking of the badness of the government" is a pastime as old as history. Like the Psalmist and the Bard, the world has always sat in judgment on its rulers.

Put not your trust in princes.

Psalm 146:3

Mad world! Mad kings! mad composition!
William Shakespeare (1564-1616)
King John

Kings is mostly rapscallions.

Mark Twain (1835-1910)

If, as Longfellow asserts,

Lives of great men all remind us
We can make our lives sublime.

they also remind us that great leaders frequently have feet of clay. It may be a degree of comfort to contemporary politicians to realize that few of them have been reviled in such sweeping terms as some of the outstanding figures of history. Men such as George Washington and Thomas Jefferson have become near-deities; but in their own times they were just politicians, fair game for criticism. The man who was to become known as The Father of His Country was reviled by his contemporaries as:

The man who is the source of all the misfortunes of our country.

William Duane (1760-1835)
On George Washington

> *That dark designing sordid ambitious vain proud
> arrogant and vindictive knave.*
>
> Gen. Charles Lee (1731-1782)
On George Washington

The American press, then as now unimpressed by their
chief executive, editorialized sonorously:

> *If ever a nation was debauched by a man, the
> American nation has been debauched by Washing-
> ton. ...If ever a nation was deceived by a man, the
> American nation has been deceived by Washing-
> ton.*
>
> Benjamin F. Bache (1769-1798)
Aurora

Washington was despaired of —

> *...and as to you, sir, treacherous in private
> friendship ... and a hypocrite in public life, the
> world will be puzzled to decide whether you are an
> apostate or an imposter, whether you have aban-
> doned good principles, or whether you ever had
> any?*
>
> Tom Paine (1737-1809)
On George Washington

and told to mend his ways —

> *If you could for a short time ... condescend to that
> state of humility, in which you might hear the real
> sentiments of your fellow citizens ... you would
> save the wreck of character now crumbling to pieces
> under the tempest of universal irritation not to be
> resisted.*
>
> William Duane (1760-1835)
Aurora

before death brought him the honor which has since been
his.

> *... the immortal leader of the American armies to
> independence, George Washington, lately deceased.*
>
> *Aurora* 1799

Thomas Jefferson, the sainted author of the Declaration

of Independence, was denounced by one of his fellow founding fathers:

> *The moral character of Jefferson was repulsive. Continually puling about liberty, equality and the degrading curse of slavery, he brought his own children to the hammer, and made money of his debaucheries.*
>
> Alexander Hamilton (1757-1804)

while a future president considered him:

> *... a slur upon the moral government of the world.*
>
> John Quincy Adams (1767-1848)
> On Thomas Jefferson

and another political opponent made the judgment that he was:

> *...a mean-spirited, low-livered fellow ... there could be no question he would sell his country at the first offer made to him cash down.*
>
> Anonymous
> On Thomas Jefferson

Jefferson's election as President was viewed with apprehension:

> *Murder, robbery, rape, adultery and incest will be openly taught and practised, the air will be rent with the cries of distress, the soil soaked with blood, and the nation black with crimes. Where is the heart that can contemplate such a scene without shivering with horror?*
>
> *The New England Courant*
> On the election of Thomas Jefferson 1800

Extravagant abuse was not the sole province of revolutionary democracies; a whole succession of English monarchs has been roundly cursed, some in detail —

> *... a pig, an ass, a dunghill, the spawn of an adder, a basilisk, a lying buffoon, a mad fool with a frothy mouth ... a lubberly ass ... a frantic madman ...*
>
> Martin Luther (1483-1546)
> On Henry VIII

some succinctly —

> *Cursed Jezebel of England!*
>
> John Knox (1505-1572)
On Queen Mary I ("Bloody Mary")

and some in verse!

> *Here lies our mutton-loving King*
> *Whose word no man relies on.*
> *Who never said a foolish thing,*
> *And never did a wise one.*
>
> The Earl of Rochester (1647-1680)
On Charles II

To which Charles is said to have replied, "True, for my words are my own, but my deeds are my ministers'."

In Quebec a century later, Thomas Walker, a merchant disgruntled by the passage of the Quebec Act in 1774, thus defaced the statue of the reigning monarch, George III:

> *Behold the Pope of Canada and the English Sot.*

Even the staid Queen Victoria has not been spared by posterity:

> *Nowadays, a parlour maid as ignorant as Queen Victoria was when she came to the throne, would be classed as mentally defective.*
>
> Bernard Shaw (1856-1950)

The unlovely Hanoverian monarchs seem to have attracted more abuse than even they deserved. Few insults to royalty can match the studied insolence of Beau Brummell's remark to Beau Nash, as the latter entered on the arm of the Prince Regent, later George IV:

> *Who's your fat friend?*
>
> George "Beau" Brummell (1778-1840)

The fashionable Brummell escaped punishment, but the poet Leigh Hunt went to prison for his mild commentary on the Prince Regent:

> *A corpulent Adonis of fifty.*
>
> Leigh Hunt (1784-1859)

and the same vindictive monarch attracted this sentiment:

> *A more contemptible, cowardly, selfish, unfeeling dog does not exist than this King ... with vices and weaknesses of the lowest and most contemptible order.*
>
> Charles Greville (1794-1865)

A traditional form of political invective is verse — often anonymous doggerel. Occasionally a public figure attracts the animosity of a well-known poet, and then the luckless victim may be memorialized forever.

> *George the Third*
> *Ought never to have occurred.*
> *One can only wonder*
> *At so grotesque a blunder.*
>
> E. Clerihew Bentley (1875-1956)

> *I sing the Georges Four,*
> *For Providence could stand no more.*
> *Some say that far the worst*
> *Of all the Four was George the First.*
> *But yet by some 'tis reckoned*
> *That worser still was George the Second.*
> *And what mortal ever heard*
> *Any good of George the Third?*
> *When George the Fourth from earth descended,*
> *Thank God the line of Georges ended.*
>
> Walter Savage Landor (1775-1864)

> *A noble, nasty race he ran*
> *Superbly filthy and fastidious;*
> *He was the world's first gentleman,*
> *And made the appellation hideous.*
>
> W.M. Ptaed
> On George IV

Oliver Cromwell, England's prickly Lord Protector, received his share of abuse, although the spirit of the age did not permit the frivolity of verse. According to his own doctor, who had the benefit of a close view, Cromwell was

> *A perfect master of all the arts of simulation: who, turning up the whites of his eyes, and seeking the Lord with pious gestures, will weep and pray, and cant most devoutly, till an opportunity offers of dealing his dupe a knock-down blow under the short ribs.*
>
> George Bate (1608-1669)

Just before Cromwell's death, some of his erstwhile supporters made haste to ingratiate themselves with the future king by denouncing their leader:

> *... that grand imposter, that loathsome hypocrite, that detestable traitor, that ... opprobrium of mankind, that landscape of iniquity, that sink of sin, that compendium of baseness, who now calls himself our Protector.*
>
> Group of English Anabaptists
> To the future Charles II 1658

The judgments of posterity have been almost as harsh:

> *He lived a hypocrite and died a traitor.*
>
> John Foster (1770-1843)
> On Oliver Cromwell

> *The Curse of Cromwell on you!*
>
> Irish curse

But those who ruled were perfectly capable of returning the same coin, although the habit of command made them more succinct. Queen Elizabeth issued a peremptory threat to a wayward churchman:

> *Proud Prelate:*
> *You know what you were before I made you what you are now. If you do not immediately comply with my request, I will unfrock you, by God.*
>
> Elizabeth I (1533-1603)
> To the Bishop of Ely

and Cromwell's dismissal of the Rump Parliament was a model of brevity:

> *You have stayed in this place too long, and there is no health in you. In the name of God, go!*
>
> Oliver Cromwell (1599-1658)

*Reader, suppose you were an idiot; and suppose you
were a member of Congress; but I repeat myself.*
Mark Twain (1835-1910)

The developing democracy of the United States provided
a fertile field for political invective. If politicians in every
age and country have been the targets of abuse, it must be
admitted that they initiated a large percentage of it
themselves. The rough and tumble of partisan politics
encourages political and personal animosities, many not
entirely genuine. It was sometimes useful to pursue them:

> *There is not a man in the United States so perfectly
> hated by the people of my district as yourself. You
> must therefore excuse me. I must abuse you, or I
> shall never get re-elected.*
Anonymous member of Continental Congress
To Josiah Quincy

In the early days of the United States Congress, the
House of Representatives was dominated by the scathing
tongue of John Randolph of Roanoak, Virginia, whose
verbal onslaughts became legendary.

> *Never was ability so much below mediocrity so well
> rewarded; no, not even when Caligula's horse was
> made a consul.*
John Randolph (1773-1833)
On Richard Rush

He is like a carving knife whetted on a brickbat.

John Randolph (1773-1833)
On Ben Harden

Randolph was not only venomous but brilliant; witness this memorable and devastating image:

> *He was a man of splendid abilities but utterly corrupt. Like rotten mackerel by moonlight, he shines and stinks.*

John Randolph (1773-1833)
On Edward Livingstone

Randolph was widely reputed to be sexually — though not verbally — impotent, a circumstance that brought forth this attack from Tristam Burges, a representative from Rhode Island:

> *Sir, divine providence takes care of his own universe. Moral monsters cannot propagate. Impotent of everything but malevolence of purpose, they can no otherwise multiply miseries than by blaspheming all that is pure and prosperous and happy. Could demon propagate demon, the universe might become a pandemonium; but I rejoice that the Father of Lies can never become the Father of Liars. One adversary of God and man is enough for one universe.*

Tristam Burges
On John Randolph

Stung, Randolph replied:

> *You pride yourself upon an animal faculty, in respect to which the slave is your equal and the jackass infinitely your superior.*

John Randolph (1773-1833)

During the course of a lengthy speech, Randolph was hectored by a representative from Ohio, Philomen Beecher, who kept popping up to cry "Previous question, Mr. Speaker, previous question!" Irritated, Randolph finally brained the gnat:

> *Mr. Speaker, in the Netherlands a man of small capacity with bits of wood and leather will, in a few*

> *moments, construct a toy that, with the pressure of the finger and thumb, will cry cuckoo! cuckoo! With less ingenuity and with inferior materials, the people of Ohio have made a toy that will, without much pressure, cry "Previous question, Mr. Speaker!"*
>
> John Randolph (1773-1833)

Randolph was a hazard in casual conversation as well:

> STRANGER: *I have had the pleasure of passing your house recently.*
> RANDOLPH: *I am glad of it. I hope you will always do it, Sir.*
>
> John Randolph (1773-1833)

> HENRY CLAY: *I, sir, do not step aside for a scoundrel.*
> RANDOLPH: *On the other hand, I always do.*
>
> The two, meeting on a narrow sidewalk in Washington

Small wonder his colleagues had to seek refuge in the classics to match him:

> *His face is ashen; gaunt his whole body,*
> *His breath is green with gall;*
> *His tongue drips poison.*
>
> Ovid, quoted by John Quincy Adams (1767-1848)
On John Randolph

Looking back on these old debates, one gets a sense of the cut and thrust of early American politics, during a period when the use of words as weapons was a highly developed art.

> *This man has no principles, public or private. As a politician, his sole spring of action is an inordinate ambition.*
>
> Alexander Hamilton (1757-1804)
On Aaron Burr

> *The bastard brat of a Scotch pedlar.*
>
> John Adams (1735-1826)
On Alexander Hamilton

> *I have no doubt that I was compleatly raskeled out of my Election. I do not regret that duty to my Self to*

my Country compels me to expose such viloney ...

Davy Crockett (1786-1836)

He is, like almost all the eminent men of this country, only half educated. His morals, public and private, are loose.

John Quincy Adams (1767-1848)
On Henry Clay

He is certainly the basest, meanest scoundrel that ever disgraced the image of God — nothing too mean or low for him to condescend to.

Andrew Jackson (1767-1848)
On Henry Clay

He prefers the specious to the solid, and the plausible to the true. ... he is a bad man, an imposter, a creator of wicked schemes.

John C. Calhoun (1782-1850)
On Henry Clay

A rigid, fanatic, ambitious, selfishly partisan and sectional turncoat with too much genius and too little common sense, who will either die a traitor or a madman.

Henry Clay (1777-1852)
On John C. Calhoun

Daniel Webster struck me much like a steam engine in trousers.

Sidney Smith (1771-1845)

... the most meanly and foolishly treacherous man I ever heard of.

James Russell Lowell (1819-1891)
On Daniel Webster

Every drop of blood in that man's veins has eyes that look downward.

Ralph Waldo Emerson (1803-1882)
On Daniel Webster

The word liberty in the mouth of Mr. Webster sounds like the word love in the mouth of a courtesan.

Ralph Waldo Emerson (1803-1882)

> *The gigantic intellect, the envious temper, the ravenous ambition and the rotten heart of Daniel Webster.*
>
> John Quincy Adams (1767-1848)

The verbal vitriol that preceded the Civil War did not end with the onset of physical violence, and leading figures like Abraham Lincoln were subject to torrents of abuse even from those on their own side. That paragon of military inactivity, General George McClellan, who later ran against Lincoln, had an excessively low opinion of his commander-in-chief:

> *The President is nothing more than a well-meaning baboon. . . . I went to the White House directly after tea where I found "the original Gorilla" about as intelligent as ever. What a specimen to be at the head of our affairs now!*
>
> General George McClellan (1826-1885)
> On Abraham Lincoln

as did the press:

> *Mr. Lincoln evidently knows nothing of . . . the higher elements of human nature. . . . His soul seems made of leather, and incapable of any grand or noble emotion. Compared with the mass of men, he is a line of flat prose in a beautiful and spirited lyric. He lowers, he never elevates you. . . . When he hits upon a policy, substantially good in itself, he contrives to belittle it, besmear it in some way to render it mean, contemptible and useless. Even wisdom from him seems but folly.*
>
> New York Post

> *Filthy Story-Teller, Despot, Liar, Thief, Braggart, Buffoon, Usurper, Monster, Ignoramus Abe, Old Scoundrel, Perjurer, Robber, Swindler, Tyrant, Field-Butcher, Land-Pirate.*
>
> Harper's Weekly
> On Lincoln

The contemporary reviews of the Gettysburg Address were universally poor:

> *... an offensive exhibition of boorishness and vulgarity.*
>
> Chicago Times 1863

> *... We did not conceive it possible that even Mr. Lincoln would produce a paper so slipshod, so loose-joined, so puerile, not alone in literary construction, but in its ideas, its sentiments, its grasp. He has outdone himself. He has literally come out of the little end of his own horn. By the side of it, mediocrity is superb.*
>
> Chicago Times 1863

But the American style was gradually changing, shaped, no doubt, by the development of the country and the growing domination of men with less formal education. The balloon of pomposity tended now to be pricked, not by the rapier of sophisticated wit, but rather by more homespun pointed humor.

There are many examples of this from Lincoln; almost none of his turning on his tormentors with slashing anger. The man could turn a phrase, though:

> *He can compress the most words into the smallest ideas better than any man I ever met.*
>
> Abraham Lincoln (1809-1865)

> *His argument is as thin as the homeopathic soup that was made by boiling the shadow of a pigeon that had been starved to death.*
>
> Abraham Lincoln (1809-1865)
> On Stephen A. Douglas

> *What kills a skunk is the publicity it gives itself.*
>
> Abraham Lincoln (1809-1865)
> On slavery

The Lincoln style is best demonstrated in his exchanges with his do-nothing general, George McClellan:

> *Sending men to that army is like shoveling fleas across a barnyard — not half of them get there.*
>
> Abraham Lincoln (1809-1865)

> *If I gave McClellan all the men he asks for they*

could not find room to lie down. They'd have to sleep standing up.

Abraham Lincoln (1809-1865)

Major-General McClellan:
I have just read your despatch about sore-tongued and fatigued horses. Will you pardon me for asking what the horses of your army have done since the battle of Antietam that fatigues anything?

Abraham Lincoln (1809-1865)
Telegram to General George B. McClellan

culminating in this laconic and despairing letter:

My dear McClellan: If you don't want to use the army I should like to borrow it for a while. Yours respectfully,

A. Lincoln
Abraham Lincoln (1809-1865)

Meanwhile, the other side in the Civil War produced its own complaints:

I have been up to see Congress and they do not seem to be able to do anything, except to eat peanuts and chew tobacco, while my army is starving.

Robert E. Lee (1807-1870)

Yes, I know Mr. Davis. He is as ambitious as Lucifer, cold as a snake, and what he touches will not prosper.

Sam Houston (1793-1863)
On Jefferson Davis

Mr. Davis's project did not prosper.

That the general public, as well as the politicians, could use the tools of invective is demonstrated in these unsolicited letters:

My dear and venerable old fellow, beware how you proceed, Sir, beware, or something will come over you as a thief in the night, which may not be so agreeable.

Anonymous
Letter to John Quincy Adams

> *God damn your god damned old hellfired god
> damned soul to hell god damn you and god damn
> your god damned family's god damned hellfired god
> damned soul to hell and good damnation god damn
> them and god damn your god damned friends to
> hell.*
>
> Mr. Peter Muggins
> Letter to Abraham Lincoln

The post Civil War era produced a succession of second-rate politicians whose deficiencies were chronicled in campaign jingles and in the jibes of their enemies:

> *Blaine, Blaine,
> We gave him a pain,
> The continental liar
> From the State of Maine!*
>
> Campaign jingle 1884

During Grover Cleveland's presidential campaign he was forced to admit fathering a child out of wedlock. This indiscretion produced a sprightly opposition jingle:

> *Ma! Ma!
> Where's my Pa?
> Gone to the White House
> Ha! Ha! Ha!*
>
> Campaign jingle 1884

but did not prevent his election:

> *If there was a wire running to the Throne of Grace,
> he'd issue orders to Almighty God, remove Christ
> Jesus as a Communist and give some Massachu-
> setts Mugwump the job ...*
>
> William Cowper Brann (1855-1898)
> On Grover Cleveland

Other political aspirants met equally vindictive comments:

> *Why, if a man were to call my dog McKinley, and
> the brute failed to resent to the death the damning
> insult, I'd drown it.*
>
> William Cowper Brann (1855-1898)
> On William E. McKinley

> *... a wretched, rattle-pated boy, posing in vapid vanity and mouthing resounding rottenness.*
>
> New York Tribune
> On William Jennings Bryan 1896

The irrepressible Teddy Roosevelt was on both the giving and receiving end of a good deal of abuse:

> *McKinley has a chocolate-éclair backbone.*
>
> Theodore Roosevelt (1858-1915)
> On William E. McKinley

> *The bestial nature of the indecent horde of pirates, second storey men, porch climbers, gunmen and short card dealers who oppose me is now perfectly manifest.*
>
> Parody of a Roosevelt campaign speech

> *At 3 O'clock*
> *on Saturday afternoon*
> *Theodore ROOSEVELT*
> *WILL WALK*
> *on the*
> *WATERS OF LAKE MICHIGAN*
>
> Spurious flyer distributed at the
> Republican National Convention 1912

> *His idea of getting hold of the right end of the stick is to snatch it from the hands of somebody who is using it effectively, and to hit him over the head with it.*
>
> Bernard Shaw (1856-1950)
> On Theodore Roosevelt

The windy oratory of Warren Harding attracted sardonic criticism from his fellow politicians:

> *His speeches leave the impression of an army of pompous phrases moving over the landscape in search of an idea. Sometimes these meandering words would actually capture a straggling thought and bear it triumphantly a prisoner in their midst until it died of servitude and overwork.*
>
> Senator William McAdoo (1863-1941)
> On Warren Harding

from acid-penned columnists:

> *He writes the worst English that I have ever encountered. It reminds me of a string of wet sponges; it reminds me of tattered washing on the line; it reminds me of stale bean soup, of college yells, of dogs barking idiotically through endless nights. It is so bad that a sort of grandeur creeps into it. It drags itself out of the dark abysm of pish, and crawls insanely up the topmost pinnacle of posh. It is rumble and bumble. It is flap and doodle. It is balder and dash.*
>
> H.L. Mencken (1880-1956)
> On Warren Harding

and from one of the trendiest poets of the day.

> *the only man woman or child who wrote*
> *a simple declarative sentence with seven*
> *grammatical errors is dead*
>
> e.e. cummings (1894-1962)
> On Warren Harding

Harding's successor followed the advice of an earlier era:

> *Never make people laugh. If you would succeed in life, you must be solemn, solemn as an ass. All great monuments are built over solemn asses.*
>
> Senator Thomas Corwin
> To President James Garfield 1881

> *I think the American public wants a solemn ass as a President. And I think I'll go along with them.*
>
> Calvin Coolidge (1872-1933)

> *He looks as if he had been weaned on a pickle.*
>
> Alice Roosevelt Longworth (b. 1884)
> On Calvin Coolidge

> *How can they tell?*
>
> Dorothy Parker (1893-1968)
> On being informed that Calvin Coolidge was dead

The great days of American political invective were waning. But the thirties produced a number of colorful characters who knew how to twist the knife:

I have always found Roosevelt an amusing fellow, but I would not employ him, except for reasons of personal friendship, as a geek in a common carnival.

Murray Kempton
On Franklin Delano Roosevelt

The Vice-Presidency ain't worth a pitcher of warm spit.

Vice-President John Nance Garner (1869-1967)

A labor-baiting, poker-playing, whiskey-drinking evil old man.

John L. Lewis (1880-1969)
On John Nance Garner

I could run on a laundry ticket and beat those bums any time.

Fiorello LaGuardia (1882-1947)
Former mayor of New York

... when I call him an s.o.b. I am not using profanity but am referring to the circumstances of his birth.

Governor Huey Long of Louisiana (1893-1967)
On the Imperial Wizard of the Ku Klux Klan

Huey Long was one of the most quixotic figures of the period. His folksy description of Herbert Hoover as a "hoot owl" and Roosevelt as a "scrootch owl" was illuminating:

A hoot owl bangs into the roost and knocks the hen clean off, and catches her while she's falling. But a scrootch owl slips into the roost and scrootches up to the hen and talks softly to her. And the hen just falls in love with him, and the first thing you know, there ain't no hen.

Huey Long (1893-1935)

Long met his match in Secretary of the Interior Harold L. Ickes, who allowed that the governor was

suffering from halitosis of the intellect. That's presuming Emperor Long has an intellect.

Harold L. Ickes (1874-1952)

Ickes was a deceptively soft-footed individual who could razor an opponent with his dry wit:

> *The General is suffering from mental saddle sores.*
> Harold L. Ickes (1874-1952)
> On General Hugh S. Johnson

He was celebrated for his description of Wendell Willkie as

> *a simple barefoot Wall Street lawyer*
> Harold L. Ickes (1874-1952)
> On Wendell Willkie

and for his needling of the brash young Republican presidential candidate, Thomas Dewey. He greeted the announcement of Dewey's candidacy with the comment:

> *Dewey has thrown his diaper into the ring*
> Harold L. Ickes (1874-1952)

and confided, about a Dewey speech:

> *I did not listen because I have a baby of my own.*
> Harold L. Ickes (1874-1952)
> On Thomas E. Dewey

His private opinion of Dewey was more devastating:

> *He is small and insignificant and he makes too much of an effort, with his forced smile and jovial manner, to impress himself upon people. To me he is a political streetwalker accosting men with "come home with me, dear".*
> Harold L. Ickes (1874-1952)
> On Thomas E. Dewey

*

The postwar era brought vast changes to the American political scene, and the old style of political vituperation is no longer in fashion. Television has removed all traces of preoccupation with language, and the fine-tuning of words is no longer an instinct. More and more the press assumes the role of political scourge, while the politicians, preoccupied with their "image" and carefully ghost-written, mince their words.

I always voted at my party's call,
And I never thought of thinking for myself at all!

W. S. Gilbert (1836-1911)

It was in the British House of Commons that the art of verbal slaughter became most highly developed. The physical, adversary layout of the House, with the ministers of the day compelled to answer for their deeds, created a cockpit atmosphere; and the educational system and the society of England put a high premium on verbal facility. One of the earliest recorded wits of the House was Richard Brinsley Sheridan, the famous playwright of *The Rivals* and *The School for Scandal*. His daily conversation in and out of the House had the same sparkle as his plays:

> *The Right Honourable Gentleman is indebted to his memory for his jests and to his imagination for his facts.*
>
> Richard Brinsley Sheridan (1751-1816)
> On the Earl of Dundas

> SHERIDAN *(leading his victim into a trap): Where, oh where shall we find a more foolish knave or a more knavish fool than this?*
> ONE HONOURABLE GENTLEMAN: *Hear, hear!*
>
> Richard Brinsley Sheridan (1751-1816)

Sheridan was also the consummate master of the fully blown image and the sustained torrent of invective.

> *They send all their troops to drain the products of industry, to seize all the treasures, wealth and*

prosperity of the country. Like a vulture with their harpy talons grappled into the vitals of the land, they flap away the lesser kites and they call it protection. It is the protection of the vultures to the lamb.

Richard Brinsley Sheridan (1751-1816)
On the East India Company

His crimes are the only great thing about him, and these are contrasted by the littleness of his motives. He is at once a tyrant, a trickster, a visionary and a deceiver. . . . he reasons in bombast, prevaricates in metaphor, and quibbles in heroics.

Richard Brinsley Sheridan (1751-1816)
On Warren Hastings

The dominant figure of the nineteenth-century House was Benjamin Disraeli. The quintessential outsider, Disraeli won his way to the top by sheer brilliance; his incomparable way with words was a major factor in his success.

Disraeli first rose to prominence by single-handedly destroying the leader of his own Conservative party, Sir Robert Peel. Peel, like many a politician before and since, campaigned against his opponents' policy — in this case, free trade — and once in office, reversed himself and adopted that policy holus-bolus. In a series of scathing speeches, Disraeli flayed Peel and ultimately forced a new election, which the Conservatives lost; Disraeli, however, won his seat and the moral leadership of the party.

The Right Honourable Gentleman caught the Whigs bathing, and walked away with their clothes. He has left them in the full enjoyment of their liberal possession and he is himself a strict conservative of their garments.

Benjamin Disraeli (1804-1881)
On Sir Robert Peel

The Right Honourable Gentleman's smile is like the silver fittings on a coffin.

Benjamin Disraeli (1804-1881)
On Sir Robert Peel

*The Right Honourable Gentleman is reminiscent of
a poker. The only difference is that a poker gives off
occasional signs of warmth.*

Benjamin Disraeli (1804-1881)
On Sir Robert Peel

Disraeli's guns were then turned on the Liberals:

*If a traveller were informed that such a man was the
Leader of the House of Commons, he might begin to
comprehend how the Egyptians worshipped an
insect.*

Benjamin Disraeli (1804-1881)
On Lord John Russell

*You owe the Whigs a great gratitude, my Lord, and
therefore I think you will betray them. For your
Lordship is like a favourite footman on easy terms
with his mistress. Your dexterity seems a happy
compound of the smartness of an attorney's clerk
and the intrigue of a Greek of the lower empire.*

Benjamin Disraeli (1804-1881)
To Lord Palmerston

The contrast between Disraeli's sparkling wit and
Gladstone's earnest pomposity could not have been more
striking.

*Mr. Gladstone speaks to me as if I were a public
meeting.*

Queen Victoria (1819-1901)

He has not a single redeeming defect.

Benjamin Disraeli (1804-1881)
On William Ewart Gladstone

*He made his conscience not his guide but his
accomplice.*

Benjamin Disraeli (1804-1881)
On William Ewart Gladstone

Even Gladstone's supporters sometimes found him intolerable.

I don't object to the Old Man's always having the

*ace of trumps up his sleeve, but merely to his belief
that God Almighty put it there.*

Henry Labouchère (1798-1869)
On William Ewart Gladstone

Asked to distinguish between a misfortune and a
calamity, Disraeli quipped:

*If Gladstone fell into the Thames, that would be a
misfortune, and if anybody pulled him out that, I
suppose, would be a calamity.*

Benjamin Disraeli (1804-1881)

In the House of Commons Disraeli delivered this perfect
parody of Gladstone's own style:

*A sophistical rhetorician, enebriated with the
exuberance of his own verbocity, and gifted with an
egotistical imagination, that can at all times
command an interminable and inconsistent series
of arguments, malign an opponent and glorify
himself.*

Benjamin Disraeli (1804-1881)
On William Ewart Gladstone

Disraeli's attacks on Gladstone continued to the end. In
his last, uncompleted novel, Disraeli caricatured the
young Gladstone:

*He was essentially a prig, and among prigs there is
a freemasonry which never fails. All the prigs spoke
of him as the coming man.*

Benjamin Disraeli (1804-1881)
On William Ewart Gladstone

The Irish agitator, Daniel O'Connell, was a particular
bête noire of Disraeli, who once denounced him as

*a systematic liar and a beggarly cheat; a swindler
and a poltroon. ... He has committed every crime
that does not require courage.*

Benjamin Disraeli (1804-1881)
On Daniel O'Connell

Sidney Smith had his own solution for O'Connell:

The only way to deal with such a man as O'Connell

is to hang him up and erect a statue to him under the
gallows.

Sidney Smith (1771-1845)

Disraeli's wit was visited on a wide range of targets:

He is a self-made man, and worships his creator.

Benjamin Disraeli (1804-1881)
On John Bright

He was the most conceited person with whom I have
ever been brought in contact, although I have read
Cicero and known Bulwer Lytton.

Benjamin Disraeli (1804-1881)
On Charles Greville

As I sat opposite the Treasury Bench, the Ministers
reminded me of one of those marine landscapes not
very unusual on the coasts of South America. You
behold a range of exhausted volcanoes, not a flame
flickers on a single pallid crest, but the situation is
still dangerous. There are occasional earthquakes
and ever and anon the dark rumbling of the sea.

Benjamin Disraeli (1804-1881)
On the Liberal ministry

Thomas Carlyle, himself noted for remarkable venom,
was at last moved to cry out against Disraeli:

How long will John Bull allow this absurd monkey
to dance on his chest?

Thomas Carlyle (1795-1881)
On Benjamin Disraeli

The Chamberlains formed one of the prominent English
political families of the late nineteenth and early
twentieth centuries. Joseph, the father, was a controversial minister in both Liberal and Conservative adminis-
trations; his sons were Austen and Neville — the first
famous as an advocate of the League of Nations, the
latter infamous as the Man of Munich. Throughout the
years, all three members of the family attracted their
share of criticism:

To have betrayed two political leaders — to have

wrecked two historic parties— reveals a depth of infamy never previously reached, compared with which the thugs of India are as faithful friends and Judas Iscariot is entitled to a crown of glory.

John Burns (1858-1943)
On Joseph Chamberlain

Mr. Chamberlain loves the working man; he loves to see him work.

Winston Churchill (1874-1965)
On Joseph Chamberlain

He always played the game and he always lost it.

Winston Churchill (1874-1965)
On Austen Chamberlain

He looked at foreign affairs through the wrong end of a municipal drainpipe.

Winston Churchill (1874-1965)
On Neville Chamberlain

He has the lucidity which is the by-product of a fundamentally sterile mind. ... Listening to a speech by Chamberlain is like paying a visit to Woolworth's; everything in its place and nothing above sixpence.

Aneurin Bevan (1897-1960)
On Neville Chamberlain

In the depths of that dusty soul there is nothing but abject surrender.

Winston Churchill (1874-1965)
On Neville Chamberlain

As Disraeli dominated the House in the nineteenth century, so Winston Churchill dominated it with words in the twentieth, although for much of that time his was a political voice in the wilderness.

I remember, when I was a child, being taken to the celebrated Barnum's Circus, which contained an exhibition of freaks and monstrosities; but the exhibit on the programme which I most desired to see was the one described as "The Boneless Wonder." My parents judged that the spectacle

*would be too revolting and demoralizing for my
youthful eyes, and I have waited fifty years to see
The Boneless Wonder sitting on the Treasury
Bench.*

Winston Churchill (1874-1965)
On Ramsay MacDonald

A curious mixture of geniality and venom.

Winston Churchill (1874-1965)
On Herbert Morrison

The Happy Warrior of Squandermania.

Winston Churchill (1874-1965)
On Lloyd George

A sheep in sheep's clothing.

Winston Churchill (1874-1965)
On Clement Attlee

A modest little man with much to be modest about.

Winston Churchill (1874-1965)
On Clement Attlee

The unassuming Attlee occasionally responded in kind:

*Fifty percent of Winston is genius, fifty percent
bloody fool. He will behave like a child.*

Clement Attlee (1883-1967)
On Winston Churchill

The spare, ascetic figure of Sir Stafford Cripps was a
favorite target for Churchill and others.

There but for the grace of God goes God.

Winston Churchill (1874-1965)
On Stafford Cripps

*He delivers his speech with an expression of injured
guilt.*

Winston Churchill (1874-1965)
On Stafford Cripps

*Sir Stafford has a brilliant mind — until it is made
up.*

Lady Violet Bonham Carter (1887-1969)
On Stafford Cripps

The election to power of the Labour Party after the Second

World War established new battle lines in the British House of Commons.

> *They are not fit to manage a whelk-stall.*
> Winston Churchill (1874-1965)
> On the British Labour Party

> *The Tories always hold the view that the State is an apparatus for the protection of the swag of the property owners. ... Christ drove the money-changers out of the temple, but you inscribe their title deed on the altar cloth.*
> Aneurin Bevan (1887-1960)

> *Here is a pretty prospect — an endless vista of free false teeth with nothing to bite.*
> Robert Boothby (b. 1900)
> On the National Health Service and continued austerity

Churchill's main challenger in the House during and after the Second World War was the peppery Welsh socialist, Aneurin (Nye) Bevan.

> *I welcome this opportunity of pricking the bloated bladder of lies with the poniard of truth.*
> Aneurin Bevan (1897-1960)
> On Winston Churchill

> *He will be as great a curse to this country in peace, as he was a squalid nuisance in time of war.*
> Winston Churchill (1874-1965)
> On Aneurin Bevan

> *He never spares himself in conversation. He gives himself so generously that hardly anybody else is permitted to give anything in his presence.*
> Aneurin Bevan (1897-1960)
> On Winston Churchill

It was not only on Churchill that Bevan turned his guns. Others on both sides of the House felt the rough edge of his tongue:

> *Please don't be deterred in the fanatic application of your sterile logic.*
> Aneurin Bevan (1897-1960)
> To fellow Socialists

... a dessicated calculating machine.

> Aneurin Bevan (1897-1960)
> On Hugh Gaitskill

A squalid, backstairs, third-rate Tammany Hall politician.

> Aneurin Bevan (1897-1960)
> On Herbert Morrison

The juvenile lead.

> Aneurin Bevan (1897-1960)
> On Anthony Eden

Why should I question the monkey when I can question the organ grinder?

> Aneurin Bevan (1897-1960)
> Preferring to question the Prime Minister, Churchill,
> rather than the Foreign Secretary, Eden

To a fellow M.P. who complained of an unending round of fraternal society luncheons and dinners, Bevan snapped:

You're not an M.P., you're a gastronomic pimp!

> Aneurin Bevan (1897-1960)

Nye Bevan, however, was usually seen by his contemporaries as a gadfly, a noisy nuisance, rather than as a major figure.

He enjoys prophesying the imminent fall of the capitalist system and is prepared to play a part, any part, in its burial — except that of a mute.

> Harold Macmillan (b. 1894)
> On Aneurin Bevan

Although the rivalry of the Harolds, Macmillan and Wilson, did not compare in verbal fireworks with the Churchill-Bevan or Disraeli-Gladstone bouts, it did have its moments:

He has inherited the streak of charlatanry in Disraeli without his vision, and the self-righteousness of Gladstone without his dedication to principle.

> Harold Wilson (b. 1916)
> On Harold Macmillan

If Harold Wilson ever went to school without any boots, it was merely because he was too big for them.

Harold Macmillan (b. 1894)
On Harold Wilson

*

As in the United States, recent decades have seen a decline in the level of British political vitriol. But this level is still higher than that across the Atlantic, and there are occasional flashes of lightning.

... an overripe banana, yellow outside, squishy in.

Reginald Paget
On Anthony Eden

Greater love hath no man than this, that he lay down his friends for his life.

Jeremy Thorpe (b. 1929)
On a savage Macmillan cabinet shuffle

He is forever poised between a cliché and an indiscretion.

Harold Macmillan (b. 1894)

*

The notorious Profumo scandal provided the impetus for a verbal sally in the old style. An attack on Profumo by the rotund Lord Hailsham, a friend of the miscreant, provoked this searing commentary:

From Lord Hailsham we have had a virtuoso performance in the art of kicking a friend in the guts. When self-indulgence has reduced a man to the shape of Lord Hailsham, sexual continence involves no more than a sense of the ridiculous.

Reginald Paget

*

What have you done? cried Christine,
You've wrecked the whole party machine.
To lie in the nude may be rude,
But to lie in the House is obscene.

Anonymous doggerel
Widely quoted during the Profumo affair

THE Canadians

> *What a country! Here all the knaves grow rich and the honest men are ruined.*
>
> Louis Joseph, Marquis de Montcalm (1712-1759)

Montcalm's early assessment set the tone for future political discussion in Canada. Although the struggles of settling a vast unpopulated territory might sometimes mute the cries of battle, there was never any question that Canadians would view their politicians and those who governed them with the same sour distaste as their British and American cousins.

One of the earliest Canadian political conflicts revolved around the fight to loosen British colonial rule and throw off the control of the ultraconservative Chateau Clique in Lower Canada and the Family Compact in Upper Canada. The views of these worthies were best represented by the doughty Archdeacon John Strachan:

> *Nobody would ask for the vote by ballot but from gross ignorance; it is the most corrupt way of using the franchise.*
>
> The Rev. John Strachan (1778-1867)

Whenever an advocate of reform managed to get elected to the Assembly, Strachan demanded his expulsion:

> *The law! the law! Never mind the law! toorn him oot, toorn him oot!*
>
> The Rev. John Strachan (1778-1867)
> Urging the dismissal of Barnabas Bidwell

One Colonial governor, Sir Peregrine Maitland, advised his successor that

> *men who were notoriously disloyal, and whose characters are really detestable are now degrading the legislature of the country by their presence.*
>
> Sir Peregrine Maitland (1777-1854)

The firebrand of the Reformers in Upper Canada was a bantam fighting-cock, William Lyon Mackenzie.

> *He is a little red-haired man about five feet nothing and extremely like a baboon, but he is the O'Connell of Canada.*
>
> John Langton (1808-1894)
> On William Lyon Mackenzie

> *... a singularly wild-looking little man with red hair, waspish and fractious in manner, one of that kind of people who would not sit down content under the government of an angel. ... he seems intent only on picking holes in other men's coats.*
>
> The Hon. Amelia Murray
> On William Lyon Mackenzie

> *... a broken-down pedlar and a notorious disturber of the public mind.*
>
> Sir Francis Bond Head (1793-1875)
> On William Lyon Mackenzie

Extreme in their views, bombastic and stubborn, the fiery Mackenzie and the incredibly inept Governor Francis Bond Head had also in common their diminutive size:

> *Afraid to look me in the face, he sat, with his feet not reaching the ground, and with his countenance averted from me, at an angle of about 70 degrees; while, with the eccentricity, the volubility, and indeed the appearance of a madman, the tiny creature raved in all directions about grievances here, and grievances there.*
>
> Sir Francis Bond Head (1793-1875)
> On William Lyon Mackenzie

Although too small to fill the chair, his shoulders

*and the poise of his head did much to counterbal-
ance the lack of nether proportions. His feet, though
unable to touch the floor, were not allowed to dangle
but were thrust out stiffly in front.*

Robina Lizars
On Sir Francis Bond Head

No love was lost between the two:

*He is, without exception, the most notorious liar in
all our country. He lies out of every pore in his skin.
Whether he is sleeping or waking, on foot or on
horseback, talking with his neighbours or writing
for a newspaper, a multitudinous swarm of lies,
visible, palpable, and tangible, are buzzing and
settling about him like flies around a horse in
August.*

Sir Francis Bond Head (1793-1875)
On William Lyon Mackenzie

In the *Colonial Advocate,* Mackenzie heaped burning
coals on the heads of the Family Compact, collectively
and individually:

*I had long seen the country in the hands of a few
shrewd, crafty, covetous men under whose manage-
ment one of the most lovely and desirable sections
of America remained a comparative desert.*

William Lyon Mackenzie (1795-1861)
On the Family Compact

*... a demon ... a hypocrite ... the Governor's
jackal.*

William Lyon Mackenzie (1795-1861)
On the Rev. John Strachan

His Majesty's butcher and baker.

William Lyon Mackenzie (1795-1861)
On John Beverley Robinson and John Strachan

*Their mothers came to America to try their luck and
were purchased by their sires with tobacco according to the quality of the article.*

William Lyon Mackenzie (1795-1861)
On the Robinson family

Mackenzie characterized Sir Peregrine Maitland as

> *one of the lilies of the field; he toils not, neither does he spin.*

and delighted in mocking the governor's ceremonial removal from his summer to his winter residence:

> *the migration from the blue bed to the brown.*

Small wonder that his victims snarled in return:

> *Another reptile of the Gourlay breed has sprung up among us. What vermin!*
>
> John Beverley Robinson (1795-1863)
> On William Lyon Mackenzie

Mackenzie castigated those who held power, and in an extravagant mixture of irony and vitriol urged his readers to action:

> *The most extraordinary collection of sturdy beggars, parsons, priests, pensioners, army people, navy people, place-men, bank directors, and stock and land jobbers ever established to act as a paltry screen to a rotten government.*
>
> William Lyon Mackenzie (1795-1861)
> On the Legislative Council

> *Tories! Pensioners! Placemen! Profligates! Orangemen! Churchmen! Brokers! Gamblers! Parasites! allow me to congratulate you. Your feet are at last on the people's necks.*
>
> William Lyon Mackenzie (1795-1861)

The mounting controversy came to a head in the comic-opera Rebellion of 1837, which its opponents chose to regard as

> *... the enterprise of a few vain, vicious, feather-brained men; it had neither spirit nor substance, deriving what poor strength it had from enemies of England ... in America.*
>
> Sir John W. Fortescue (1859-1933)

Mackenzie became a temporary outlaw, and his name

was henceforth a controversial one for Canadian reformers. The alarmed British government sent Lord Durham to investigate the situation, unwittingly founding a new industry and inaugurating a classic Canadian method for postponing an issue — the Royal Commission of Inquiry. Durham was unimpressed with what he found:

> *Not government merely, but society itself seems to be almost dissolved; the vessel of the State is not in great danger only, as I had been previously led to suppose, but looks like a complete wreck.*
>
> Lord Durham (1792-1840)

Durham produced a report which earned him the nickname "Radical Jack" and, like every Royal Commission report since, was both hailed and condemned:

> *It is a farrago of false statements and false principles ... the most fatal legacy that could have been bequeathed to our American colonies.*
>
> *Quarterly Review* 1839

> *Lord Durham's plan is* English, *and directly tends to raise a nation of equal and prosperous freemen; the plan of his opponents is* Russian, *and directly tends to produce a few arrogant, insufferable nobles, and a multitude of wretched, insulted slaves.*
>
> *Upper Canada Herald,* Kingston 1839

Durham's report was accepted and the Canadian colonies lurched toward self-government and ultimate unity. A driving force in the move toward federation, and the dominant Canadian politician of the second half of the nineteenth century, was John A. Macdonald, a Kingston lawyer whose uncanny resemblance to Disraeli went more than skin deep. His ability to lead, prod, cajole, compromise and scheme was largely responsible for the Act of Confederation in 1867; he was Canada's first Prime Minister, and despite scandals and disenchantments he was out of office for only brief periods until his death in

1891. His political demise was often predicted — always prematurely:

> *Sir John A. Macdonald is about to retire to private life, a thoroughly used-up character.*
>
> Toronto *Globe* 1858

Like all successful Canadian political leaders, Macdonald was adroit at delaying issues until they somehow solved themselves or quietly went away. His habits of procrastination earned him a sobriquet that dogged him the rest of his life:

> *"Old Tomorrow" would be just the name for Sir John.*
>
> Col. A.G. Irvine (1837-1916)

His political wiliness led to mixed feelings in more than one opposition M.P.—

> *Ah, John A., John A., how I love you! How I wish I could trust you!*
>
> Anonymous Liberal M.P. 1863

Some of the judgments on him were ambiguous, to say the least:

> *Had he been a much worse man he would have done Canada much less harm.*
>
> Sir Richard Cartwright (1835-1912)

But most observers were more inclined to marvel at his resilience:

> *Well, John A. beats the devil!*
>
> Luther Holton (1817-1880)
On Macdonald's reelection following the Pacific Scandal

Macdonald was frequently exasperated by political opponents. An early example was Sir Oliver Mowat, later Liberal premier of Ontario.

> *You damned pup. I'll slap your chops for you!*
>
> Sir John A. Macdonald (1815-1891)
To Oliver Mowat in Ontario House of Assembly

One of Macdonald's chief opponents in the Confederation negotiations was

> *That pestilent fellow, Howe.*
>
> Sir John A. Macdonald (1815-1891)
> On Joseph Howe

Joseph Howe was a Nova Scotia publisher and leader of a valiant fight for freedom of the press, who seldom minced his words. He was at first an enthusiastic supporter of Confederation:

> *Let the dog return to his vomit rather than Canada to division.*
>
> Joseph Howe (1804-1873)
> To Confederation conference

but whether out of principle, or for other motives,

> *I will not play second fiddle to that damned Tupper.*
>
> Joseph Howe (1804-1873)
> Declining to attend Charlottetown and Quebec Conferences

Howe boycotted the negotiations and became bitterly opposed to the scheme. The pro-Confederation forces were scornful of the doubters:

> *Prince Edward Island will have to come in, for if she does not we will have to tow her into the St. Lawrence.*
>
> Thomas D'Arcy McGee (1825-1868)

Howe weighed in on the other side, dubbing the new plan 'The Botheration Scheme''.

> *Messrs. Tupper, Archibold and McCully when the deed is done, may escape to Canada and stifle, as Arnold did, the reproofs of conscience amidst the excitements of a wider sphere and of more lucrative employment. But what is to become of the poor dupes who have been their accomplices in this dark transaction? Nineteen-twentieths of them will live and die at home, and all their lives must behold the averted faces of their indignant countrymen; and creep at last to dishonoured graves in the bosom of*

*the province they have betrayed, to poison the
worms that consume them beneath the soil to which
they were untrue.*

Joseph Howe (1804-1873)
"The Botheration Papers"

When, ignoring Howe, the Legislature voted to enter
Confederation, Nova Scotia became entitled to a grant of
80¢ per capita as part of the bargain.

We are sold for the price of a sheepskin.

Joseph Howe (1804-1873)

*LITTLE BOY: Father, what country do we live in?
FATHER: My dear son, you have no country, for Mr.
Tilley has sold us all to the Canadians for eighty
cents a head.*

Andrew R. Wetmore (1820-1892)
Imaginary dialogue with his son

John A. Macdonald led the Conservatives for nearly
forty years; during that time he faced a succession of
leaders of the Clear Grits, or Liberals, as the reform party
came to be known. Preeminent among these was George
Brown, editor of the *Globe,* an irascible, Jovian figure
who played Gladstone to Macdonald's Disraeli:

After some five minutes' conversation in the Globe
*office with a hungry-looking bald-headed individu-
al in his shirt sleeves, and nails in mourning, I
desired to see the Honourable Brown himself. Much
to my surprise I found that he stood before me.*

Horton Rhys 1861

*The great reason why I have been able to beat
Brown is that I have been able to look a little ahead,
while he could on no occasion forego the temptation
of a temporary triumph.*

Sir John A. Macdonald (1815-1891)
On George Brown

Sir John was able to turn his well-known penchant for the
bottle into a weapon against the unbending Brown:

I know enough of the feeling of this meeting to know

*that you would rather have John A. drunk than
George Brown sober.*

> Sir John A. Macdonald (1815-1891)
> Election speech

A later Prime Minister, for fifteen years, was the elegant,
sophisticated Wilfrid Laurier.

*That damn dancing-master who had bitched the
whole show.*

> Dr. S. Jameson (1853-1917)
> To Rudyard Kipling, on Sir Wilfrid Laurier

*A man who had affinities with Machiavelli as well
as with Sir Galahad.*

> John W. Dafoe (1866-1944)
> On Sir Wilfrid Laurier

*I would rather do business with a cad who knows
his own mind.*

> Joseph Chamberlain (1836-1914)
> On Sir Wilfrid Laurier

Laurier did not have an excessively exalted view of his
fellow countrymen:

*The great mass of the electors are ignorant, and a
great majority of them never read, and remain as
much in the dark as to what is going on in this
country as if they were residing in Europe.*

> Sir Wilfrid Laurier (1841-1919)
> To Edward Blake

*Had I been born on the banks of the Saskatchewan,
I would myself have shouldered a musket to fight
against the neglect of governments and the shame-
less greed of speculators.*

> Sir Wilfrid Laurier (1841-1919)
> On the hanging of Louis Riel

Laurier fell out with his party over the conscription issue
during the First World War, and all but a handful of
Liberals abandoned him. When he died four years later,
the unseemly scramble of his erstwhile followers to do
him honor prompted one sardonic onlooker to comment:

> *Do you think we can trust the bastards with the old man's body?*
>
> Charles Murphy (1863-1935)

Nineteenth-century Canadian politics threw up a number of strong personalities, many of them connected with the building of the Canadian Pacific Railway. Donald Smith, later Lord Strathcona, incurred the displeasure of Macdonald:

> *I could lick that man Smith quicker than hell could frizzle a feather.*
>
> Sir John A. Macdonald (1815-1891)
> On Donald Smith

It was an age when neither politicians nor press hesitated to call a spade a spade:

> *He was so flattered and fondled by great men in high offices, that he looked as bewildered with unexpected honours as an interesting young widow giving herself away in matrimony for the fourth time.*
>
> On Amos Wright, M.P.P.

> *How many Canadian M.P.P.s could obtain third-class certificates from the most lenient of our educational examination boards?*
>
> R.J. Macgeorge (1811-1884)
> *Streetsville Weekly Review*

> *The Fisherman who would sell Bait to a Frenchman would steal the pennies off his dead mother's eyes.*
>
> Newfoundland political placard
> During fishing dispute with France 1886

> *He has but one principle, that of self-interest. He has only one desire, the desire to insult. He belongs to the school of lying, hypocrisy and cowardice.*
>
> E.E. Cinq-Mars
> On Sir George Foster 1906

See the faces of the Grits,
Grizzly Grits,

What a woe-begone expression at
present o'er them flits.

But the people — they who vote —
of their twaddle take no note,
For they know the dismal, dreary,
direful dole
Of the Grits
Of the moribund, morose and melancholy
Grits, Grits, Grits, Grits,
The greedy, grubby garrulous old Grits.

The People's Almanac 1891

*The mud-bespattered politicians of the trade, the
party men and party managers, give us in place of
patriotic statecraft the sordid traffic of a tolerated
jobbery. For bread, a stone. Harsh is the cackle of
the little turkey-cocks of Ottawa, fighting the while
as they feather their mean nest of sticks and mud,
high on their river bluff.*

Stephen Leacock (1869-1944)

Canadian political discussion in the middle years of the
twentieth century was conducted in much less acid terms,
partly due to the long prime ministerial tenure of William
Lyon Mackenzie King. Grandson of the old Reformer,
King was the antithesis of his ancestor — cautious,
shrewd, equivocal and the ultimate compromiser. He
enveloped his listeners in a fog of words, through which
his political intentions were barely discernible. Curious-
ly, this outwardly dull man brought out the poet in his
critics, at least one of whom pounced on the personal
eccentricities revealed only after his death.

He skilfully avoided what was wrong
Without saying what was right,
And never let his on the one hand
Know what his on the other hand was doing.

Frank Scott 1957
On W.L. Mackenzie King

William Lyon Mackenzie King
Sat in the middle and played with string;

And he loved his mother like anything —
William Lyon Mackenzie King.

Dennis Lee 1974

Despite its rather bland exterior, politics in Canada has remained lively enough in this century; the advent of two new political parties, the early activities for women's rights, and a number of flamboyant politicians have ensured that.

The way to get things out of a government is to back them to the wall, put your hands to their throats, and you will get all they have.

Agnes McPhail (1890-1954)
First woman elected to the Canadian Parliament

I am opposed by all the short-haired women and the long-haired men in the Province.

Sir Rodmond Roblin (1853-1937)

I just hold my nose and mark the ballot.

Frank Underhill
Asked how he could vote Liberal 1967

Those people in Ottawa couldn't run a peanut stand.

W.A.C. Bennett
Former premier of British Columbia 1967

I don't mind someone stealing my pyjamas, but he should wear all of them if he doesn't want to appear indecent.

T.C. Douglas
Former premier of Saskatchewan,
On Liberal appropriation of CCF (NDP) policies 1971

For socialists, going to bed with the Liberals is like having oral sex with a shark.

Larry Zolf 1975

The left in Canada is more gauche *than* sinister.

John Harney 1970

Social Credit once had a war on poverty. Phil Gaglardi started to throw rocks at beggars.

Graham Lead
Former B.C. Minister of Highways 1975

Corporate Welfare Bums!
NDP campaign slogan 1972

No shirt is too young to be stuffed.
Larry Zolf
On Conservative leader Joe Clark 1977

Former Prime Minister John Diefenbaker's zest for parliamentary debate is legendary, and he was always at his best when criticizing. Both the despised Grits and members of his own party, who later deposed him, have felt his verbal lashes:

> *The Liberals are the flying saucers of politics. No one can make head nor tail of them and they never are seen twice in the same place.*

*

> *When I think of some of the statements made here I begin to think that we are living in a new age of palaeontology — political palaeontology — the invertebrate age, which is government without a backbone.*

*

> *If I were a Roman Catholic, the first thing I would do every morning would be to get down on my knees and ask my God for absolution for ever having appointed McCutcheon to the Senate.*
On Wallace McCutcheon, a fellow Conservative

*

> *... that adjectival authority, pusillanimous and uncertain as he pictures the darkness spreading over Canada.*
On Lester B. Pearson

*

> *Jean Lesage is the only person I know who can strut sitting down.*
On the former Premier of Quebec

*

> *Flora MacDonald is the finest woman to have walked the streets of Kingston since Confederation.*
On a rival Conservative

John G. Diefenbaker (b. 1895)

*

I couldn't have called him an s.o.b. — I didn't know he was one — at the time.
John F. Kennedy (1917-1963)
On John G. Diefenbaker

For ten years the Canadian public has carried on a love-hate relationship with the enigmatic Pierre Trudeau.

> *The Hon. Member disagrees. I can hear him shaking his head.*
>
> Pierre Elliott Trudeau (b. 1919)

> *When they get ten steps away from the House of Commons, they are nobodies.*
>
> Pierre Elliott Trudeau (b. 1919)
> On opposition M.P.s

> *In Pierre Elliott Trudeau Canada has at last produced a political leader worthy of assassination.*
>
> Irving Layton (b. 1912)

On one famous occasion, the Prime Minister was accused of "mouthing" the ultimate obscenity in the House. Inspiration striking, Trudeau insisted that the actual phrase was

> *Fuddle-duddle!*
>
> Pierre Elliott Trudeau (b. 1919)

and a disbelieving but amused nation took up the new expression with enthusiasm.

*

Canadians continue to be preoccupied with the century-old concern of political independence:

> *Ours is a sovereign nation*
> *Bows to no foreign will*
> *But whenever they cough in Washington*
> *They spit on Parliament Hill.*
>
> Joe Wallace 1964

*

The last word on the Canadian Parliament was found in the pocket of a critic whose bomb, intended for the Commons chamber, exploded prematurely:

> *Mr. Speaker, Gentlemen, I might as well give you a blast to wake you up. . . . The only bills you pass are the ones that line your pockets, while the rest of the country has to eat spaghetti and meat balls.*
>
> Paul Joseph Chartier 1966

The Temper of Democracy

The essence of democratic politics is the right to participate, and the citizen can take a vigorous role in criticizing as well as choosing his rulers. The elected politician has to hone his wit on the often arduous campaign trail. In the sometimes rough, sometimes humorous interchange with hostile voters, a quick mind is a precious asset:

> CONSTITUENT: *Vote for you? I'd as soon vote for the devil!*
> JOHN WILKES: *And if your friend is not standing?*
>
> *
>
> HECKLER: *Speak up, I can't hear you.*
> DISRAELI: *Truth travels slowly, but it will reach even you in time.*
>
> *
>
> VOICE IN CROWD: *Give 'em hell, John!*
> JOHN DIEFENBAKER: *I never give them Hell. I just tell the truth and it sounds like hell to the Grits.*
>
> HECKLER: *Don't you wish you were a man?*
> AGNES McPHAIL: *Yes. Don't you?*
>
> *
>
> HECKLER: *Go ahead, Al. Tell 'em all you know. It won't take you long.*
> AL SMITH: *If I tell 'em all we both know it won't take me any longer.*

But sometimes even an experienced political orator can be outmatched by that most inventive user of invective, the ordinary citizen:

EARL WARREN: *I'm pleased to see such a dense crowd here tonight.*

HECKLER: *Don't be too pleased, Governor, we ain't all dense.*

*

MITCHELL HEPBURN: *(at a farm meeting, speaking from a manure spreader) This is the first time in my life that I have spoken from a Tory platform.*

HECKLER: *Throw her in high gear, Mitch, she's never had a bigger load on.*

*

HECKLER: *I'm a Democrat!*

THEODORE ROOSEVELT: *May I ask the gentleman why he is a Democrat?*

HECKLER: *My grandfather was a Democrat; my father was a Democrat; and I am a Democrat.*

THEODORE ROOSEVELT: *My friend, suppose your grandfather had been a jackass and your father was a jackass, what would you be?*

HECKLER: *(instantly) A Republican!*

*

Despite changing styles and intermittent attempts to suppress it, the democratic right to criticize remains intact. Nor do opinions change. Compare these descriptions of two Democratic presidential conventions, a century apart:

> ...*the meanest kind of bawling and blowing office-holders, office-seekers, pimps, malignants, conspirators, murderers, fancy-men, custom-house clerks, contractors, kept-editors, spaniels well-train'd to carry and fetch, jobbers, infidels, disunionists, terrorists, mail-riflers, slave-catchers, pushers of slavery, creatures of the President, creatures of would-be Presidents, spies, bribers, compromisers, lobbyers, sponges, ruin'd sports, expell'd gamblers, policy-backers, monte-dealers, duellists, carriers of conceal'd weapons, deaf men, pimpled men, scarr'd inside with vile disease, gaudy outside with gold chains made from the people's money and harlot's money twisted together; crawling, serpentine men,*

the lousy combinings and born freedom-sellers of the earth.

Walt Whitman (1819-1892)
On a Democratic National Convention of the 1850s

*

A man of taste, arrived from Mars, would take one look at a convention floor and leave forever, convinced he had seen one of the drearier squats of Hell ... a cigar-smoking, stale-aired, slack-jawed, butt-littered, foul, bleak, hardworking, bureaucratic death gas of language and faces ... lawyers, judges, ward heelers, mafiosos, Southern goons and grandees, grand old ladies, trade unionists and finks; of pompous words and long pauses which lie like a leaden pain over fever.

Norman Mailer
On the 1960 Democratic National Convention

Plus ça change, plus c'est la même chose. What will they be saying in another hundred years?

* * * * * * * * * * * * * * *

Democracy is a form of religion. It is the worship of jackals by jackasses.

H.L. Mencken (1880-1956)

Index of Authors and Sources

Index of Subjects